How the Homosexuals
Saved Civilization

How the Homosexuals Saved Civilization

*The True and Heroic Story
of How Gay Men Shaped
the Modern World*

Cathy Crimmins

JEREMY P. TARCHER / PENGUIN
A MEMBER OF PENGUIN GROUP (USA) INC.
NEW YORK

While the author has made every effort to provide accurate telephone numbers and Internet addresses at the time of publication, neither the publisher nor the author assumes any reponsibility for errors, or for changes that occur after publication.

Most Tarcher/Penguin books are available at special quantity discounts for bulk purchase for sales promotions, premiums, fund-raising, and educational needs. Special books or book excerpts also can be created to fit specific needs. For details, write Penguin Group (USA) Inc. Special Markets, 375 Hudson Street, New York, NY 10014.

Jeremy P. Tarcher/Penguin
a member of
Penguin Group (USA) Inc.
375 Hudson Street
New York, NY 10014
www.penguin.com

Copyright © 2004 by Cathy Crimmins
All rights reserved. No part of this book may be reproduced, scanned, or distributed in any printed or electronic form without permission. Please do not participate in or encourage piracy of copyrighted materials in violation of the author's rights. Purchase only authorized editions.
Published simultaneously in Canada

Library of Congress Cataloging-in-Publication Data

Crimmins, C. E.
How the homosexuals saved civilization : the true and heroic story of how gay men shaped the modern world / Cathy Crimmins.
p. cm.
ISBN 1-58542-314-9 (alk. paper)
1. Gay men—Social life and customs.   2. Gays in popular culture.
3. Homosexuality and art.   4. Homosexuality—Philosophy.   I. Title
HQ76.C74 2004   2004049790
306.76'62'0973—dc22

Printed in the United States of America
1 3 5 7 9 10 8 6 4 2

This book is printed on acid-free paper. ∞

Book design by Lovedog Studio

If you removed all of the homos and homo influence from what is generally regarded as American culture, you would be pretty much left with *Let's Make a Deal*.

—Fran Lebowitz

To all my gay boyfriends—especially
the fabulous St. James Shatzer

As always, to the memory of John Gaggin

And, finally, to the memory of Matthew Shepard, and
in celebration of two friends who survived brutal attacks,
Robert Drake and Trev Broudy

Contents

Book One
Heart

Book Two
Body

Book Three
Soul

Homosexuals have pinned their intergration into society on promoting the aesthetic sense.

—Susan Sontag

Toto, I've a feeling we're not in Kansas anymore.
—Dorothy Gale (played by Judy Garland)
in *The Wizard of Oz*

Putting My Finger on It

I grew up in paradise. The area had every natural resource going for it—rolling green hills, a gentle scenic river, heirloom trees, and views of endless fields and woods dotted with wild and domestic animals. But it wasn't the natural setting that spelled paradise to me. Even as a child, I leaned more toward artificial pleasures, which the place had in droves. The pretty valley skirting the Delaware River boasted flamboyant restaurants in eighteenth-century inns, fine local theater that attracted actors, writers, and directors from New York and Hollywood, quaint antiques shops, art galleries, and impossibly beautiful garden stores.

Growing up in Bucks County, Pennsylvania (or, actually, right over the river in New Jersey, in Hunterdon County), was wonderful because intrepid gay pioneers had come before us, blazing a trail filled with all the important things in life. They had settled this rural area right after World War II, and made it civilized.

As a young girl, I couldn't put my finger on what made the area around New Hope, Pennsylvania, so fabulous, so different from other rural or suburban environs. Now I know that it was this steady presence of gay men that set it apart. The labels "homosexual," "faggot," and "queer" were never mentioned in my household. Instead, my family displayed a quiet appreciation for what at that time was a closeted culture.

In the small river town where my parents had started a company, we all admired the local florists, two well-dressed men who created the most elegant arrangements for miles around. They shared "bachelor" living quarters and kept two standard poodles in their shop. Our family went to the Lambertville Music Circus, an outdoor tent theater owned by St. John Terrell, who brought in Dorothy Lamour, Donald O'Connor, and other campy old-time stars to perform in Broadway musicals.

Before he retired to the country to stage plays in a tent, St. John Terrell had made a splash in 1933 as the original "Jack Armstrong, the All-American Boy" on radio. Now I see his early role as ironic. Outside the soundstage, Jack Armstrong was probably doing things considered to be very un-American at the time. As a kid in the sixties and seventies, I saw the flamboyant Terrell nearly every Christmas morning in the reenactment of George Washington crossing the Delaware. He took the role very seriously, standing at the bow of the boat in

the exact same position George assumes in the famous painting. After reaching shore, the bewigged and rouged Terrell
made a speech and swirled his navy blue cape. Then he made
his exit, complete with colonial drummers, flags, and a long,
slow march into the distance. It was very campy, although my
child-mind didn't see it that way. Apparently others had
caught on, though, since some time in the early seventies a
bunch of college students rented a speedboat, plastered it with
British flags, and sped around George's boat, trying to get St.
John Terrell to fall into the water. I've since learned that Terrell identified himself as heterosexual, so I guess I have to put
him in the ever-expanding "gay-seeming" category of theater
types.

Campy sites and activities were everywhere around me.
You only had to go one town over to Stockton, New Jersey, to
find the original "small hotel with a wishing well" described
by Rodgers and Hart in their famous song. Lorenz Hart, who
wrote some of the best lyrics in the world, was a tortured,
closeted gay man. Playwright Moss Hart (also allegedly a
closeted gay man) and his wife, Kitty Carlisle, had a house
nearby. Dorothy Parker had lived with her allegedly gay (bisexual?) husband, Alan Campbell, only a few miles from our
house. I wasn't surprised recently to find that Andy Warhol
had discovered Charles Rydell, the star of his movie *Blow Job,*
in a performance of *Lady in the Dark* with Kitty Carlisle at the
Bucks County Playhouse.

My family dined at Chez Odette on the canal in New Hope,
which was owned by Odette Mytril Logan, the original
Bloody Mary on Broadway in *South Pacific.* She had a piano

bar where handsome young homosexuals sang catchy tunes well into the night. (And, okay, I hate to bring it up again, but there were standard poodles running around the place, too.) I didn't know that many of the handsome men with good voices were gay—it was never discussed, but it was *there*. The gayness in the room was like the infamous elephant in the drawing room, which made an enormous impact on the environment, even if no one would admit it.

At a town north of where we lived, I auditioned to be in the chorus of a summer stock theater, where I met my first gay boyfriend. Of course I didn't exactly know that Wesley was queer (my gaydar was as yet undeveloped), but I knew enough to have on hand another, more sexually forward, beau. So while Wesley, the gay boyfriend, helped me with my stage makeup and introduced me to Cole Porter tunes, opera, and the poetry of W. B. Yeats, my less civilized, straight high-school lover had sloppy sex with me in the backseat of his car and on my parents' living-room floor. I still have the edition of Yeats's collected poetry that Wesley gave me, whereas I have nothing left of any value from my boorish straight boyfriend.

So what does all this mean? Why do I still yearn for the paradise of my youth, created mostly by closeted gay men? This early utopian vision of a world where everything was "nice" and "interesting," and never dull, has had a lasting effect on my adult choices. Because I was exposed to the homosexual aesthetic at an early age, I've never wanted to live anywhere without gay men. I enjoy being in a world where foreign cinema, tropical floral arrangements, and provocative finger foods are considered life necessities. Why wouldn't I? The straight male aesthetic often features beer and Barca-loungers.

Without the artful influence of gay men, our American landscape can seem like a wasteland, like one giant Wal-Mart, or Disney World. Would I want my daily life to resemble a bad version of Superbowl Sunday? It's too frightening to contemplate.

I've come to realize that my upbringing was a tad unusual for the times. If the topic of male homosexuality was never overtly discussed, it was at least *implied* in my household. I was exposed to a raft of unspoken positive queer stereotypes. Gay men were creative, interesting, and talented. The men who lived together or alone, who were my father's age but had no wives, had the time and money to create flair and style. My father, a beleaguered breeder, might have been wearing dorky straight plaid pants and Hush Puppies, but he got to eat in gay restaurants and attend gay theater productions.

Yet one needn't have lived in a partially gay community to have benefited enormously from the homosexual influence in the last five decades. The gay sensibility has always shaped heterosexual culture, a fact that the straight community is only now beginning to notice and admit.

Fifties housewives swooned over Montgomery Clift and Rock Hudson without knowing that they were falling in love with men who epitomized the gay aesthetic—falling in love, really, with a homosexual ideal represented in a heterosexual context. These same women bought clothes by gay designers and had their hair done by gay hairdressers. They fell in love to romantic songs composed by homosexuals. They devoured fashion magazines staffed by gay photographers and advice columnists working under female pseudonyms.

Straight people took to the soup can, Andy Warhol's pop manifesto. They were fascinated by his postmodern take on ordinary objects. How many of them even knew he was gay? I didn't.

Looking back, I can see how America fought hard to ignore the gay undertow of our culture from the fifties well into the eighties. There were so many unanswered questions. Why was Paul Lynde the funniest guy on *Hollywood Squares?* Why were Liberace's clothes and jewels the most fabulous? Why were Johnny Mathis ballads the favorite make-out music for heterosexual couples in the sixties? Why were many of the greatest playwrights of the last half of the twentieth century— Tennessee Williams, Lanford Wilson, Terrence McNally, Edward Albee—all gay men writing for straight audiences? Why are Cole Porter's love songs the cleverest and most poignant?

Back then we were struggling, as a culture with too many closets, to ignore the idea that many of our modern notions about art, romance, theater, cinema, fashion, food, and *life itself* were shaped by gay initiatives and perspectives.

Fortunately, we no longer need to be in denial. We're in a golden age of "Global Queering," in which ideas and behaviors associated with gay groups are constantly making their way into mainstream culture, whether it's a newly popular mixed drink (think martinis and cosmopolitans), a new emphasis on gossip and the cult of the celebrity (the E! red carpet broadcasts or Steven Cojocaru's ultra-gay fashion tips on the *Today* show), or a precise and scrupulous way of looking at the human form (Bruce Weber's homoerotic billboards for upscale underwear).

And now, in our new century, straight America is embracing gayness in a dizzy, lovestruck way. The summer of 2003 will always be remembered as the moment when straight America came out of its closet and finally extended a Statue-of-Liberty welcome to gay immigrants. The Fab Five on *Queer Eye for the Straight Guy* thrilled us with their makeovers while reality TV extended its sexuality to include *Boy Meets Boy.* Pundits everywhere made up lists of what was gay and what was not. Is this just a phase? Worse, is it just a kind of pandering condescension? Are gay guys the newest pop-culture flavor? Is America just overcompensating for its rampant homophobia by adopting gay mascots in the movies and on television? Do straight folks yearn to wear "gay-face" the way guilty racists wanted to don blackface at the beginning of the last century?

No, I believe that the "gay thing" is here to stay. What we're seeing now is just the tip of the cultural iceberg. They're here, they're queer, and straight America is getting used to it. Hell, we're even appreciating it.

"Mom, am I a hag-fag?" said my daughter when she was nine years old.

"That's fag-hag!" I snapped back. *Gee,* I thought, *I hate that word, and now I'm teaching it to her in its correct form.*

I used to resist being typed as a fag-hag. I originally intended to write a long, angry section about how this is not a book by a fag-hag. I love gay men, unabashedly. But the label "fag-hag" has always stung. Fag-hags are supposed to be women who can't get a straight man of their own, who hang around gay guys on whom they have crushes. The fag-hag is the absolute bottom in a very complex emotional relationship. She lives vicariously through the achievements of her "fag." The fag-hag is a major symbol of unrequited love and failed femininity.

Yet I can't help being in awe of gay men and their cultural accomplishments. I want to celebrate them and bring them to America's attention. So I've decided that I don't care if I come across as the biggest fag-hag in the land. And if the word "queer" can be redeemed and given dignity, then why not "fag-hag"?

Fag-hag. Yes, I am one. Fag-hag, *c'est moi*. "Fag-hag" will one day be a friendly label, and I do think it is due for rehabilitation. The comedian Margaret Cho has already begun its repositioning. "I am fortunate enough to have been a fag-hag for most of my life," she writes in her book, *I'm the One That I Want*.

The term "stag-hag" to describe a heterosexual male who is friendly to gays has already emerged, so can the elevation of fag-hag be far behind? (And I'm waiting for "hag" to pass into the suffix category, as "queen" has. If we can have a drama queen, how about a "flag-hag" for a righteous right-winger, or "mag-hag" for someone who's overly into *Us* or *Vogue*?)

How the Homosexuals Saved Civilization is not specifically about chronological gay history—there are many tomes that cover that. I don't have any interest in identifying who was homosexual and who was not throughout recorded time. There will be no revelatory "Hitler was a fag" or "Lincoln was gay" moments here.

In discussing gay men's influence on straight culture, I've focused mostly on post-Stonewall culture (meaning the period after 1969, after the Stonewall riots in Greenwich Village, the event that most historians cite as the beginning of the gay rights movement), although some of my examples go as far back as the 1930s.

Unfortunately, for the most part I've excluded lesbian culture: However hard their struggle, lesbians have tended to be more domestic, making less of an impact on cutting-edge trends in our culture than gay men have. This, too, will probably change.

I've tried hard not to succumb to the Bermuda Triangle of Queer Theory, the academic discipline that views all culture through the lens of gay alienation and identity. Although I admire this research, I detest its jargon. I have no intention of boring you with long linguistic or theoretical digressions. *How the Homosexuals Saved Civilization* is a work of love from a fag-hag author. This book celebrates how an unusual "immigrant" group, homosexual men, has become the latest and most astonishing influence on mainstream American culture.

The Three
Civilized Books:
Heart, Body, and Soul

There's nowhere to run,
I have no place to go,
Surrender my heart, body, and soul

—Backstreet Boys,
"Show Me the Meaning of Being Lonely"

Every culture has three components: heart, body, and soul. If we are to see how dramatically mainstream American culture has been influenced by male homosexuality, we must look at all of the components of the gay culture.

Heart is that culture's very way of thinking, its emotional core. How does this group of people see the world and internalize it? How does it communicate its ideas? What is most important to the people of this culture—what is "gut level," or at its heart? What are its rituals and celebrations?

1

Body is the way in which a culture addresses the fundamentals of life: food, shelter, and sexual activity. What is the native cuisine? How do the citizens adorn their homes? What do they wear? What constitutes the culture's sense of the physical body, of sexuality and sexual roles, and what are its sexual practices?

Finally there is soul, or the spiritual essence of a culture, expressed in its art, literature, drama, and music. What distinguishes this culture's thoughts about life and death? How is its art expressed, and what are the most popular forms? How have the culture's arts been influenced, and how do they influence other societies and groups?

Here, then, are the heart, body, and soul of influential gay culture. Here are the gifts gay culture has brought to straight civilization.

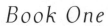

Book One

Heart

Chapter 1

I Know It
When I See It:
Camp, Irony, and the
Gay Aesthetic

Camp is a certain mode of aestheticism. It is one way of seeing the world as an aesthetic phenomenon. That way, the way of Camp, is not in terms of beauty, but in terms of the degree of artifice, of stylization.

—Susan Sontag, "Notes on Camp"

In fact, queerness is so pervasive ... that it prompts the question: What's left that's truly hetero?

—Simon Dumenco, *New York Magazine*

Some years ago, New York's New Museum sponsored a forum called "Is There a Gay Sensibility and Does It Have an Impact on Our Culture?" After a lot of evasive huffing and puffing about everyone from Marcel Proust to Patti Page, journalist Jeff Weinstein said, "No, there is no such thing as a gay sensibility and yes, it has an enormous impact on our culture."

—Vito Russo, *The Celluloid Closet*

Defining the gay aesthetic is difficult. It's particularly tricky when discussing artists or thinkers who were "pre-homosexual," existing in cultures in which homosexuality was not thought of as a lifestyle but as an occasional sexual option. Countless books and articles have been written on the probable homosexuality of Leonardo Da Vinci, Michelangelo, Shakespeare, and Tchaikovsky. I had a lively conversation with a gay history professor about this topic. We agreed that it was silly to label artists as homosexual before the term or concept even existed. (The word "homosexual" was coined in 1869 but did not catch on as a term for decades. It was first uttered in a public forum on a BBC broadcast in 1953.) So how can we anachronistically interpret artists' works, burdening them with a "gay" label, when in fact in their day and time what they did with their bodies at night probably had nothing to do with the way they lived daily? Leonardo da Vinci, who even in liberal Florence was prosecuted for homosexual acts, would have been considered a sodomite, but that definition would have carried moral, not social, connotations.

Yet there is a certain gay sensibility in the works of painters such as da Vinci and Michelangelo. "I can definitely feel that gayness emanating from their art," said the history professor. It's as difficult to pin down what seems gay in, say, an old *I Love Lucy* episode or a forties Joan Crawford movie. When it comes to identifying a gay aesthetic, I feel forced to quote Supreme Court Justice Potter Stewart's famous line about what constitutes pornography: "I know it when I see it."

You'd think that it would get easier with more recent history, but that's not the case. Many famous arbiters of taste and style, and indeed many of the artists we now call gay, would not have labeled themselves as such and would not appreciate being outed, even after death. Many of these men married and had children. Consider, for example, Leonard Bernstein, Malcolm Forbes, or Danny Kaye.

"How to Be Gay: Male Homosexuality and Initiation," a course taught by Professor David M. Halperin in the English department at the University of Michigan, Ann Arbor, caused a ruckus in the conservative press in 2003. The course description neatly touches on aspects of the gay aesthetic: "This course will examine the general topic of the role that initiation plays in the formation of gay male identity. . . . In particular, we will examine a number of cultural artifacts and activities that seem to play a prominent role in learning how to be gay: (including) camp, diva-worship, drag, muscle culture, taste, style and political activism."

A gay sensibility "tends to be clever, scornful of laws, introspective, energetic and sexy," says Rick Whitaker, author of *The First Time I Met Frank O'Hara: Reading Gay American*

Writers. I would add that the gay aesthetic also arises from an extreme sense of alienation, with a bit of narcissism thrown in for good measure. When one is alienated from the mainstream life and must create a protective niche and a common means of recognizing those who are similarly alienated, a full other set of customs, language, and art can arise. The culture of closeted gay men before the 1970s was underground but thriving; once the events of the Stonewall riots in Greenwich Village in 1969 forced Americans to an awareness of homosexuality itself, it also made us more aware of the gay sensibility, the gay sense of humor, and the gay insistence on camp and irony. Of course, as everyone eventually discovers about the best things in life, the gay sensibility had been there all along.

Straight People Who Think Gay

Can you be straight and have a gay sensibility? I would argue yes. As gay attitudes spill over into straight culture, the gay aesthetic pops up in entertainment phenomena and other places. Boy bands such as 'N Sync and the Backstreet Boys, for example, have a whiff of the gay about them, as teen idols of other eras have had, too. (The straight 1950s teen idols Frankie Avalon and Fabian were both discovered by a gay manager.)

The beleaguered Martha Stewart, a straight woman, has done almost as much as anyone to promulgate the gay design aesthetic for heterosexual Middle America. Both straight and gay people will say, "That's sooooo Martha!" A friend of mine calls Martha Stewart "the gayest man I know." Thousands of gay men watch Martha's broadcasts and keep every issue of her magazine, yet she has also introduced a new taste in flowers (no more dreadful heterosexual carnations!) and in home décor to housewives and working women all across the country. This melding of gay aesthetic and heterosexual domestic longings has been going on for a long time.

Even in casual conversation outside of gay environments, people will rate how "gay" something is. One night Conan O'Brien and actor Jason Schwartzman discussed the various hair products they use to tame their locks. "How gay is this conversation, anyway?" O'Brien remarked to his straight guest. It was more a comment about aesthetics than sexuality. In this age of Global Queering, many of our cultural obsessions with celebrity, body image, hair, and fashion stem from homosexual attitudes as surely as Venus rose from the half shell in Botticelli's famous painting.

Three Things About Gay/Straight Culture

Here are a few things I've learned about searching for the gay sensibility:

1. *Elton John was right: There is a Circle of Life.*
Sir Elton, a famously once-closeted, now openly gay man, wrote the lyrics for the song "Circle of Life," featured in the

Disney animated film *The Lion King,* and later more lyrics for the famous Broadway show of the same name, which many homosexual as well as straight families attended. The song describes the inevitable Circle of Life, and it might as well be describing the inevitable transfer of gay trends to straight culture: "It's the leap of faith/It's the band of hope/Till we find our place/On the path unwinding."

Time and again, as I examined the influence of gay men and the homosexual sensibility on straight life and rituals, I saw a circle, a straight-to-gay-to-straight-again circle. Things that seem heterosexual were once gay; likewise, many factors of culture that seem gay were once straight. I'm thinking earrings on rednecks, boys in baggy cargo shorts, Methodist picnics with pesto. The Circle of Life poignantly identifies how much gay culture has influenced our daily lives

The Circle of Life approach can be a helpful template for seeing how trends move back and forth through what can only be described as the permeable membrane of American culture.

Likewise, there is an American Circle of Life when it comes to trends. The trendiest trends pass from those who have been most marginalized in society—from gays, blacks, Asians, and other minorities to the more mainstream straight, white-bread culture. And when something overtly homosexual or incredibly cool comes on the scene, there is always a progression from the gay audience to the female audience to the straight male/female, or "breeder," audience.

Ted Allen, the food stylist on *Queer Eye for the Straight Guy,* described this very same progression of awareness to the

Chicago Tribune in talking about how he and the rest of the Fab Five first started getting noticed in public.

> *First it was the gay guys in Chelsea. . . . And right about the same time, it was the single women. Then we started hearing from ladies my mother's age, you know, around 60. Now we're starting to get high school boys and college guys, straight guys, in airports coming up to us and saying, "Dude, thanks for that shaving tip, man."*

2. There is always the Tallulah Factor.

Although it might be apocryphal, I've always loved a famous Tallulah Bankhead line, much quoted in gay circles. When asked if one of her husbands had been gay, Tallulah said, "I don't know. He never sucked my cock."

There's a difficulty in tracking who was what, and who did what to whom. There are so many obviously gay guys who have never come out of the closet, and so many closeted gay men who maintain marriages. How can one ever really determine a sexual orientation? And are the nitty-gritty details of a person's sex life all that important?

For the most part, I have decided to identify as gay any man who has been consistently outed in several sources, even if that man spent his life married to a "devoted" female spouse. But I've also learned much about the gay sensibility from the literature, music, and art of men who have refused to be identified as gay but definitely embody or embrace the gay sensibility.

3. The Liberace Syndrome may always be invoked.

Like all straights, I have suffered from the Liberace Syndrome, a failure to acknowledge something totally gay even when it slaps me in the face. Many Americans born before 1960 have this problem. Even Liberace himself seems to have suffered from it. He sued a London newspaper once for saying he was homosexual. (And for those of you born *way* past 1960, let me tell you that Liberace was a flamboyantly gay Las Vegas performer. He played the piano really well, and wore white suits with sequins. He was like Siegfried or Roy without the tigers.)

It's almost embarrassing, looking back, to see how much Americans denied the gay inflections of our society. The Liberace Syndrome continues today in pockets throughout our nation, and especially in the elderly population.

Gay Men and the Irony Epidemic

Gay men have provided heterosexuals with caustic, exaggerated visions of our sexuality and gender roles. They have taken what has seemed familiar and comfortable to us and turned it on its ear. It is impossible now to see *Leave It to Beaver* or *The Brady Bunch* without snickering at the silliness of the average straight family. Can anyone watch a Joan Crawford movie and not think *Mommy Dearest?* The martini, long a 1960s suburban staple designed to ease the homecoming of the weary heterosexual breadwinner, passed out of popularity, only to be revived in gay bars and given new life with rather precious ingredients (apple, chocolate, etc.). And now, of course, Middle America has embraced with gusto this "new" trend of elaborate mixed cocktails.

It is tempting to see gay men as the canaries of culture, out there ahead, breathing in dangerous new trends before they catch on with the rest of the population. But this is too passive a way of thinking about the enormous impact of gay sensibility on popular culture. Gay men *create* trends, and straight people are damn lucky that an "immigrant" group with such a fine aesthetic sense is out there on the vanguard, providing a new way of approaching every aspect of our daily lives.

What Is Gay? Applying the Lenny Bruce Rule

In the sixties, the comedian Lenny Bruce performed a brilliant routine about what is Jewish and what is gentile, or goyish. He took the concept of being Jewish beyond ethnicity, and beyond literal definition:

Dig: I'm Jewish. Count Basie's Jewish. Ray Charles is Jewish. Eddie Cantor's goyish . . . Marine corp—heavy goyim, dangerous. Kool-Aid is goyish. All Drake's Cakes are goyish. Pumpernickel is Jewish, and, as you know, white bread is very goyish. . . . Trailer parks are so goyish that Jews won't go near them. Underwear is definitely goyish. Balls are goyish. Titties are Jewish. Mouths are

Jewish. All Italians are Jewish. Greeks are goyish—
bad sauce. Eugene O'Neil—Jewish; Dylan Thomas,
Jewish . . .

Bruce goes on to say that if you live in New York City, even if you're a Christian, you are Jewish, and that if you're Jewish and reside in Butte, Montana, you are still a goy. His routine is a true comedy classic because it gets laughs by defining ethnicity as part of a larger cultural environment. To be Jewish is to share certain tastes and preferences—it has nothing to do with religious beliefs.

His flexible definitions transfer perfectly to "gayness." If you're straight and live in Provincetown, Massachusetts, Key West, or West Hollywood, you are gay, whatever your sexual preference. If you live in Midland, Michigan, you're going to be straight, no matter how many same-sex encounters you have daily or weekly. All actors are gay, whereas all civil engineers are straight. Interior decorators are homos; dentists are hets.

Defining a gay aesthetic is tricky. This is the place where stereotypes collide with valid observations. You can say that iceberg lettuce is straight and arugula is gay, but of course there are many gay men who adore iceberg lettuce for its real self, and then others who love it for its ironic effect in hip restaurants where it's served in wedges with blue cheese and bacon. Likewise, many straight people live for arugula salads. But in the end, iceberg is straight, arugula is gay—no doubt about it.

Yet I, a straight woman, have an obsession with arugula. But it doesn't count, because growing up in a rural area, I was introduced to arugula under the name of "rocket salad." How dorky is that? How straight is that?

A young gay man once tried to explain to me why army was straight and navy was gay. "The navy has cuter uniforms. They're not butch, like army fatigues. The navy pants make the guys' asses look good. The navy guys are away for a long time, in close quarters together. And then of course there's the obvious 'cruise' metaphor."

The gay/straight lists of things thread through our culture, forming the yin and yang of American society. Tennis is gay; golf is straight. Wrestling is gay; football is straight. Steak is straight; grilled chicken is gay. Poodles are gay; Labrador retrievers are straight. Scottish tartans are straight; Burberry tartan (in its most recent incarnation) is gay. Disco is gay; rock is straight. Opera is gay, gay, gay. Stock car racing is intensely straight (even if I once found a whole website devoted to gay NASCAR fans, Gaytona.com, hosted by drag queen/racing fan Betty Jack DeVine). Hunting is straight, and so are fishing and bowling.

Of course, these definitions are always shifting. Quiche was once considered an effeminate food, and now it's a staple at airport restaurants. Earrings on men were gay until blue-collar guys started adopting the look.

A female friend of mine used to play a game: straight florist, gay florist. Now, by the Lenny Bruce standard, *all* florists would be gay. But when my friend (who had many operations) was lying in her hospital bed, it was easy for her to tell immediately the origins of the floral arrangements that arrived in her sickroom. The straight ones *always* contained carnations and scruffy mums and other boring flowers. Even arriving at varied heights and textures seemed to be a major challenge for the straight florists. So what made the gay bouquets so wonderful? They were fragrant, hip, tropical, and amazing in their juxtaposition of perennials and exotic filler material, such as tropical grasses and twisted woods.

One time I ate in a cheap Italian restaurant in Philadelphia with terrible décor. One major wall was sponge-painted in coarse circles of two mismatched hues. My dining partner (a straight woman) said it before I could: "Gosh, I've never seen heterosexual sponge painting before."

I have a friend, a floral designer, whose tastes perfectly reflect the gay aesthetic. Before he was a designer, he was a chef, and before that, a window dresser for a major department store. He practiced this last profession while he was married—his marriage lasted seventeen years, and he says he will always be in love with his wife, "only she is the wrong sex." This friend, St. James, has the most highly honed gay aesthetic I've ever encountered. Everything he does is impeccable, from the perfect potato pancakes he cooks for his Jewish Hanukkah dinner clients (he is a goy) to the beautiful Christmas packages he wraps and distributes each year. We have a joke within our social circle—we try to make up one another's epitaphs. We've already decided that St. James's epitaph will be "Wrapped Without Tape." His packages are perfectly presented, nestled in Japanese rice paper and tied with gorgeous chiffon ribbons in muted pastel hues.

I thought about these ribbons when shopping in a small tourist town with my fourteen-year-old daughter and David, a sixteen-year-old boy she calls her "gay husband." At one dress shop, David effortlessly picked out a dress for my daughter. It was black with a beautiful gored fit through the stomach and thighs. She didn't want to try it on; he insisted. The thing turned out to be a miracle garment—the little black dress you would discover in utopia. It made her look fifteen pounds lighter, sophisticated, and trim. We bought it. "I found you this dress," said David, "so I have fulfilled my function as a gay man." Then he giggled.

In a gift shop, we came upon a display of the exact same chiffon ribbons my friend St. James uses for his perfect packages. Actually, we didn't come upon them—David saw them and drew us over. "I love these!" he said, fluttering his hands toward the display. I started to say that my friend used the same ones, but then stopped: What does it matter? They are exquisite ribbons, and I can't imagine any straight boy even noticing them. It was the gay aesthetic at work.

Ethnic "Gay" Stereotypes

An aesthetic is a shared cultural vision. Communities develop habits and tastes. We can usually make generalizations about the aesthetic sensibility of certain ethnic groups. For example, I can go into a Thai restaurant and know that there will always be fresh flowers, and probably decorative fabrics. The sets for the cable television series *The Sopranos* reflect a nouveau riche sensibility—furnishings that a wealthy Italian-American might own, such as white leather sofas, chandeliers, and mirrored rooms.

But gay men are not, officially, an immigrant group (although they are finally being counted by the U.S. census). Male homosexuals do not come from a specific place. Unlike other immigrant groups, gay men discover their cultural heritage as they grow up and discover other gay men. Sometimes this requires emigrating to urban centers or vacation towns that provide a nonthreatening atmosphere. But just as often, today and in the past, gay men have been immigrants on their own, settling within obvious heterosexual populations and exerting subtle yet notable influence.

Defining Culture, Defining Civilization

In her famous essay about "camp" and the gay aesthetic, Susan Sontag points out that Jews and homosexuals have been the two major influences on modern American culture. I would say that it is now gay men who are the primary cultural catalysts. Their cultural power, and the enormous influence they've wielded on our American tastes, is now coming into view, finally.

What is civilization? In the strictly anthropological sense, of course, it means the particular characteristics of a community at a certain time and in a certain place. But when most of us speak of a place being "civilized," we are thinking of what

Webster's calls "refinement of thought, manners, or taste." More than any other minority group, gay men have contributed the civilized aspects of our modern lifestyle, and they've done it fueled by the transforming power of alienation.

When one is outside the mainstream culture, it seems more possible to concentrate on the finer things in life—literature, art, fashion, haute cuisine, and even perfection of the human body. Gay men have offered the straight world the enormous gift of aesthetic vision.

Pundits who analyze the diversity of American culture tend to use homey metaphors. We're a melting pot of many different types of people making up the national stew, they say. We're a tapestry of various cultures woven into one richly textured American fabric. If those metaphors hold, then homosexuals, as one of the most recent "ethnic" cultures affecting the mainstream, are the spices in the melting pot. Gay men are the flamboyant bright streaks of yarn in our American tapestry.

Chapter 2

Language: Gayspeak and Straight Shooters

I bitch-slapped the law, and the law won!

—Sean Hayes as Jack on *Will & Grace*

That's Mr. Faggot to you!

—Slogan on a T-shirt sold in Greenwich Village

Movieline magazine: You're a speed queen?

Courtney Cox Arquette: I'm heavy on the pedal, yeah.

—Interview in the January 2003 issue, in which the *Friends* star talked about loving her car

Straight people who want to seem hip tend to talk like gay guys. Of course, there's no way we pathetic breeders can compete with the linguistic talents of homosexual men, but we try. Inevitably, the gayspeak that shows up in our dull, mainstream lives sounds as flat as a bottle of San Pellegrino that's been left with its cap off for two days.

Sometimes, though, we don't even know that the phrases we are suddenly so taken with have gay origins. I'm amazed by how often that happens in modern life—words and phrases get picked up and lose their original meaning or context. Just one example that is neither straight nor gay: A lawyer friend once got a goofy look on his face and said, "The dingo ate my baby!" I then commented about *A Cry in the Dark*, the campy Australian movie in which an ugly-wigged, falsely accused murderess Meryl Streep utters that line. "Huh?" said my friend. It seems that he had never heard of the movie. He just liked the way the phrase sounded. He might as well have been yodeling in an Australian accent.

This happens all the time with formerly gay-only terms and phrases. A young woman says that she's a closet chocolate freak. What does she mean? "Oh, that I hide how much chocolate I eat." Further discussion reveals that she has no idea that the concept of a virtual closet was once an exclusively gay metaphor. In fact, she has no idea that to "come out" as a gay person is just a shortening of the phrase "to come out of the closet."

To "out" someone became a verbal construction in the eighties, when endless debates raged about whether it was fair to reveal someone's same-sex orientation without consultation. Now to be "outed" has a wider connotation and is often part of hetero-speak. "Please don't out me as a hamburger-lover," a male heterosexual coworker once said to me. A person can be outed for smoking or liking bad TV shows—all fairly trivial offenses compared to having to explain a sexual lifestyle in the midst of a homophobic environment.

Divine Adjectives and Modifiers

Everything is soooooooo something these days, isn't it? This formerly homosexual modifier pops up everywhere, and it's as useful as "umm" and "like" in conversations. Sometimes the "sooooo" doesn't have to modify anything—it can be accompanied by eye rolling or a fingered "loco crazy circle sign" just as effectively. Graham Norton, the sooooo gay host of a popular BBC talk program, became "So Graham Norton" for the title of his show. One use of "so" has particularly captivated straight talkers: the combination of "so" and a year, as in "so 1987" or "so 1999." Another popular phrase, "so last year," comes directly from gay fashion designers and pundits. "I am so over that" is another great put-down and all-purpose transition phrase for straight talkers, followed closely by "all that." She's all that, he's all that, we're *all* that.

"Totally" is another omnipresent gay modifier. One hears it everywhere now, and it was put to good effect in the title of VH1's clever documentary *Totally Gay*.

The way homosexual men use adjectives has transformed American speech. In the fourth grade, I wrote a story about two astronauts in a space capsule. My teacher criticized me for having one of the male astronauts say that Earth looked "gorgeous" from up above. Real men don't talk like that, she said. Girls talk like that. Now, forty years later, straight male lingo has been heavily inflected by swishy, over-the-top adjectives, and on demographically young stations such as MTV and in Gen-Y guys' magazines, formerly effeminate adjectives such as marvelous, fabulous, yummy, breathtaking, and glorious are crossing over to a straight audience.

The word "fabulous," especially, is making a huge comeback and is used by straights almost as often as gays. Of course, there's always the question of whether "fabulous" is being used seriously or in an elaborate show of irony. Since even among straight people, fabulous is often said with an elaborate drawl—Dahling, you look faaaaabuuuuulous—my guess is that the word has drifted to the land of irony, never to be redeemed. In my book, gay men invented irony, and straight Americans embraced it. Irony, especially the mainstream-culture-irony brand hawked by faux talk shows such as *The Daily Show with Jon Stewart,* has emerged as a peculiar American art form. It's different than satire, originally a purely British product.

But back to "fabulous." The British sitcom *Absolutely Fabulous (AbFab)* is about two sodden middle-aged straight women who talk like gay men. The delightful Patsy and Edina dialogues, written by the show's creator, Jennifer Saunders, complete a pop-culture cycle that has been ongoing since the 1960s, a sort of intellectual ecosystem. The two women have borrowed their locutions from gay culture (Edina's second husband actually *was* gay, and so is her son). Sweetie, darling, fabulous, fantastic—these are regular *AbFab* terms. "I simply *adore* it," Edina will say. And who are the biggest fans of these straight women spouting gayspeak? Gay men. And so the speech cycle from gay to straight back to gay again is completed, as it often is.

I spoke to Los Angeles actor Sam Pancake, who's often cast as a gay male assistant or waiter in films (*Legally Blonde 2*) and on TV shows (*Friends, Will & Grace*). Pancake is annoyed by straight people who try to talk like gays, or who think gays should talk a certain way.

"I had this one female director on a film who would rush over to me on the set and kiss me and say, 'Honey, you look fabulous! How are you, girlfriend?' Or she'd say, 'You go, girl.' None of my circle says these things. That's old stuff that only straight people would think of saying. We don't do 'she' for he. We don't call each other girlfriends. I guess she thought she was putting me at ease, or showing off her gay vocabulary. To me it's as insulting as if I were black and she sauntered over and said, 'Hey, bro, wassup?'" But the worst thing, said Pancake, was the "damned word 'fabulous.'"

"We were improvising some dialogue and she wanted me to say 'fabulous' this and 'fabulous' that. Finally I stopped and looked at her and said, 'Perhaps you've noticed that I don't say "fabulous." At all. Ever.' She backed down, and I had a modest victory. I think I ended up saying 'fantastic,' which is more of a relief than you can imagine."

Pancake was a guest star on the famous "c-word" episode of the HBO comedy series *Curb Your Enthusiasm*. In the episode, Pancake plays a seemingly straight studio executive who makes a bad call at a poker game. Larry David calls him a "cunt," and all hell breaks loose. Larry loses his chance to do a show with the network, and Pancake's character has a nervous breakdown and comes out of the closet as a gay man.

"We were trying to find a signal, supposedly a subtle one, that my character was gay before the 'cunt calling' incident happens," says Pancake. "*Curb Your Enthusiasm* is improvised from an outline, so all of us were throwing around what words would make me seem gay. A couple of the actors suggested that I compliment someone on an article of clothing made by Prada or Armani. I thought that was too stereotyped. Instead, we hit upon having me call myself a 'ditz' when I dropped some cards. All of us agreed that a straight man would never use the word 'ditz' to describe himself."

Are there words that a truly straight man would never utter? Probably. There is a funny spelling-bee episode on *Will & Grace* in which Jack is asked to spell "taffeta." Yet I like to think that straight men, and women, *are* pressured to use words they might just ignore when they are presented with them on gay-inflected restaurant menus and in Pottery Barn catalogs.

The Gay Co-opting of Multicultural Vocabulary, and God Save the Queen

Let's talk about the word "queen." Until the seventies or so, it merely meant a female ruler of a country or a particularly effeminate homosexual. The term "drag queen," indicating a homosexual man who dresses as a woman, has been around since at least the 1920s. Yet in the last decade, "queen" has developed a new meaning that has crossed over to the straight community. To be a "queen" means you are particularly intense about something.

The term that has crossed over best to heterosexual-land is "drama queen," meaning someone who adores his or her own personal drama a bit too much. A drama queen is a whiner. All teenagers make good drama queens.

In casual straight slang, a "queen" suffix can be attached to any predilection; hence Courtney Cox Arquette, who likes to drive fast, can be dubbed a "speed queen." A person who loves films can be a "movie queen." I've seen avid Internet types described as "computer queens." Yet lurking in the wings in the gay verbal community are far more sexually descriptive uses of the queen construction. Rice queen: a guy who likes Asian men. Size queen: a man who prefers large penises. Curry queen: a lover of Indian men. The term "queen" is just a great platform for instantly categorizing a person's obsessions and desires. It is endlessly versatile and ripe with future possibilities for the straight vocabulary. I predict that heterosexuals will someday refer to men who like big breasts as "boob queens."

Whereas "queen" originated in England, another popular gay term, "diva," comes from Italy. It's an opera term that gay men have made their own. They've expanded the definition, taking it from its original meaning of a great female singer to a woman who excels in other fields or even peculiar domains.

"When I was in my twenties, someone said to me, 'Your mother is a real diva, isn't she?'" says Luke Yankee, son of actress Eileen Heckart, who starred in the films *Butterflies Are Free* and the gay cult classic *The Bad Seed*, among many other movies and Broadway plays.

"I was confused," says Yankee. "How could my mother be a diva? She was an actress, not a singer." Yankee, who became a stage director and playwright, went on to work with many divas himself in the twenty years after he first learned that his mother was one. Now he says that the word means "someone who is outstanding in his or her field, and someone who can sometimes be stubborn and a perfectionist." After twenty years in the theater, he created a one-man show called Diva Dish, about his mother and her friends. In the process, he found that divas were everywhere.

"The term has definitely crossed over to the straight world. Just Google the word and you'll see it everywhere."

I did just that, and found thousands of entries. There are diet divas, wine divas, horror divas, feng shui divas, rubber-stamp divas, makeup divas, and scrapbook divas. My favorite was "dorm diva," meaning the alpha girl who has the looks and power on a college dormitory floor. But the word, after it was borrowed from the opera world, was used by gay men for years to indicate a high-maintenance person or a spectacular personality. The surest sign of its straight appeal nowadays is the array of diva specials on VH1. Cher, Tina Turner, Brandy, Aretha Franklin, Mariah Carey, Céline Dion, Gloria Estefan, Shania Twain, Diana Ross, Donna Summer, Queen Latifah, and Faith Hill have all been designated "divas" on these programs, the most popular in VH1 history.

I asked Luke Yankee about the title of his own show, *Diva Dish*. Was that particularly gay? Did he name it that because he's a gay actor/director?

"I first heard the word dish in gay circles around 1984," he said. "But now I've found that the term is very familiar to straight audiences. 'Dish' is now just a term for gossip, straight or gay. I didn't give it a second thought. Most of my audiences are straight people, on cruise boats, college campuses, and in theaters. They understand what 'Diva Dish' means immediately."

The gay community has also borrowed greatly from African-American slang, and has served as a conduit to the straight world for certain terms. I first heard "diss," now a common phrase in all circles, from my gay male friends. Yet it started in the black community as a verbal form culled from "disrespect." The term "bitch-slap" also crossed over from black speakers to the gay male world, where it has become mostly a vague threat and a colorful way to express aggression, a kind of bark without a bite. Straight folks use it, too, and they also use "slut" and "whore" in ironic ways— these two terms have lost their sting since filtered through the gayspeak context. "Girlfriend" and "You go, girl!" also made their way to the gay male world via the black urban slang lexicon, as well as everyone's new favorite put-down, "skanky ho."

Silver-Screen Speak

Gay men taught America how to become infatuated with pithy movie dialogue. Long before all of us went around saying "Show me the money!" or "Go ahead, make my day," gay men were communicating by uttering famous lines from campy cult movies. Many of these phrases have now passed into hetero-speak. "People come and go so quickly here," says Dorothy in *The Wizard of Oz*. The Oz phrase is also uttered by Prior as he lies dying of AIDS in *Angels in America*, and repeated by gay and straight people in real life when they are feeling confused or anxious. (It's interesting that from the sixties well into the eighties, gay men would ask one another "Are you a friend of Dorothy?" a parody of the Alcoholics Anonymous question "Are you a friend of Bill?")

Big-eyed Bette Davis, in various roles, was a fount of campy lines embraced by gay men and then later by heterosexuals. "Fasten your seatbelts, it's going to be a bumpy night," she says in the campy classic *All About Eve*. "What a dump!" she screams in *Beyond the Forest*. And, in a more subdued mood, she utters a line that will be said ironically by gay men for decades: "Oh Jerry, we have the stars, let's not ask for the moon." (*Now, Voyager*)

Another favorite line of gay men that has become more universal comes from Blanche DuBois in *A Streetcar Named Desire:* "I've always relied on the kindness of strangers." Of course, Blanche was created by a gay playwright, Tennessee Williams, and many gay men saw themselves in Blanche's vulnerability, promiscuous sexuality, and loneliness. Yet in the last decade I've heard more straight people than gay people use this line in conversation.

In one of the final episodes of *Sex and the City*, Charlotte's gay designer friend Anthony does the movie-line tradition proud by introducing a new generation of cinematic reference. Charlotte (Kristin Davis) tells Anthony (Mario Cantone) that her new dog, Elizabeth Taylor, is ready to compete at dog shows even if her former owner didn't appreciate her qualities. "Nobody puts Baby in the corner!" says Anthony. When Charlotte doesn't get the reference, Anthony explodes: "*Dirty Dancing!* Helloooooo!"

Homo-Wit: The Power of Description

Is there a more descriptive elocution in the whole world than "gaydar"? This combination of "gay" and "radar" cap-

tures perfectly the fun and the stress of being a gay man trying to connect with someone. Is your gaydar working, or will
you be rebuffed? There is no straight equivalent, and yet I
hear heterosexual women use the word more and more if they
are worried that a man they're trying to seduce is really not
playing for their team.

"Breeder" is another great gayspeak term. Recently I've
heard married couples refer to themselves that way. Homosexuals used to deride the breeder lifestyle. Yet the word
"breeder" has suddenly become the "faggot" or "queer" of
the straight world, a derogatory word now embraced. It's become less loaded, like a synonym for a soccer mom or dad.
Ironically, too, children have become the newest accessory for
gay men, so they've become breeders themselves in greater
numbers. (I eagerly await what stylistic and psychological in-
novations gay men will bring to parenthood. I'm sure they'll
raise kids with more flare than their heterosexual counterparts.)

Yet why stop at one-word coinage? Gayspeak inspires
everyone to wittier locutions. The narrative of our lives is becoming richer because gay men supply striking verbal versions of visual images. Who can beat Noel Coward's seemingly
effortless comment, "She stopped the show—but then the
show wasn't traveling very fast."

People tune in to *Queer Eye for the Straight Guy* as much for
the banter as they do for the fashion makeovers. Carson
Kressley, the skinny blond, is the series wit. He has a snappy
comment about almost everything. Seeing one hapless victim's long boxer shorts, Kressley quips that he should be
churning butter in colonial Williamsburg. "Clothes tell a story,"

he tells another young man, "and yours tell the story of a crazy, deranged kickboxer who still lives with his mother in Queens."

I was surfing the Net and found myself on a gay man's blog in which he painstakingly rated *all* the fashions worn on TV reality shows. He referred to one contestant in a yellow shirt as "Matt Damon–tasty." Gayspeak is descriptive and exaggerated at the same time. The queer celebrity gossip Michael Musto described himself in one column as "looking like a cow flop." Asked about the artist formerly known as Prince, Boy George opined, "He looks like a dwarf who's been dipped in a bucket of pubic hair."

A friend told me about a very effeminate gay man she adored who walked into a bar, not knowing it served a rather rough leather crowd. He immediately puffed himself up, pulled up a barstool, and said, "Bring me something pink, and make it snappy!"

One instant-wit verbal game created and played by gays and then passed on to straight people is the "your porno-star name" game. (I've also heard it described as the "your stripper name" game.) The game is a great conversation-starter at parties. All a person has to do is combine the name of his or her first pet with the name of the first street he or she lived on. My gay porno name is "Skippy Conover." I like it. It's kind of manly/slutty.

Before he came out as a gay man, actor Nathan Lane was frequently asked about his sexual orientation. At several interviews, he said, "Look, I'm forty, I'm single, and I work in mu-

BUSINESS REPLY MAIL

FIRST-CLASS MAIL   PERMIT NO 419   RED OAK IA

POSTAGE WILL BE PAID BY ADDRESSEE

Reader's Digest

PO BOX 8064
RED OAK IOWA 51591-3064

NO POSTAGE
NECESSARY
IF MAILED
IN THE
UNITED STATES

PREFERRED
GIFT DISCOUNT VOUCHER

	Annual Cover Price:	Gift Subscription Rate:	Annual Discount Savings Off Cover Price:
	$35.88	$27.98 Plus state tax, if any.	22%

Send my Reader's Digest Gift Subscription to:

NAME _____ APT#

ADDRESS _____

CITY _____ STATE ___ ZIP ___

Bill me $27.98 for 12 issues, plus state tax if applicable:

NAME _____ APT#

ADDRESS _____

CITY _____ STATE ___ ZIP ___

SEND NO MONEY NOW — WE'LL BILL YOU LATER.

22 % SAVINGS

NPBNSAOL

Reader's Digest

The Reader's Digest Association, Inc.

ACCESS NO.:

122659 1023 5426

COURTESY RATE:

12 issues / $27.98

SAVINGS OFF COVER PRICE

22%

12/2798

sical theater—you do the math!" That bitchy, clever answer is the gayest thing he's ever said, although after he officially came out, he followed it with nearly as clever a quip during a television interview: "Even now, I don't greet people by saying, 'I'm Nathan Lane, and I'll be your homosexual.'"

The straight streak of witty gay talk began with Oscar Wilde: "Always forgive your enemies; nothing annoys them so much." Today Wilde's mantel has been inherited by David Sedaris, one of the wittiest writers in America, who is gay but has a huge straight following on National Public Radio. His radio bits and published essays are gems of sardonic wisdom that display the full range of gay-language sensibility.

Says Sedaris, "'College is the best thing that can ever happen to you,' my father used to say, and he was right, for it was there that I discovered drugs, drinking, and smoking."

In a brilliant essay about his lisp, Sedaris talks about being forced to spend hours in therapy with other little gay boys. The sign on the door of the speech lab "might as well have read Future Homosexuals of America," he writes. He also has the gay gift of poignant coinage—his beautiful essay "The Youth in Asia" is all about how his family had to put their dog down.

With an audience of both educated gay and straight people on NPR and exposure in mainstream publications such as *Esquire* and *The New York Times*, Sedaris is improving the vocabulary of heterosexuals just as surely as Cole Porter provided witty romantic lines for straight couples in his songs.

Dirty Talk: The Future of Gayspeak's Influence on the Straight World

Linguists and speech therapists study an aspect of language called "code switching," the ability of a person from a closed group to change diction, inflection, and vocabulary when talking to someone from another group. The best, and simplest, example of code switching occurs when adults talk to babies or small children. Our voices become higher and more melodic, and we use nonsense words or very simple sentences. Foreign-language speakers also code-switch as they go from language to language.

Gay men have code-switched for years, keeping their style of speaking and their vocabularies out of their conversations with straight people. Yet as acceptance of homosexuality heightens, there is less code switching going on. The straight world has already benefited from the influx of gay terms and locutions. And now we are on the cusp of the final linguistic frontier: dirty talk!

Terms such as "fuck buddy," "trick," and "boy toy," which describe a more casual attitude toward sexual relationships, are already making their way into straight parlance. (*Sex and the City* devoted a whole episode to the fuck-buddy concept: a casual friend to whom you turn for sex on a fairly regular basis.) The gay term for checking out potential sexual partners, "to cruise," has also been appearing in the heterosexual lexicon.

Several decades ago, to say "You suck!" or "This sucks"

in public was forbidden. Now it's a regular mode of discourse heard on nightly talk shows, and many people have forgotten that the object of the verb "suck" was once "cock" or "dick," and that the phrase once had distinctly homosexual connotations.

The verb "to butt-fuck" is now an established heterosexual phrase. It's rampant in bad heterosexual teen movies, where it always gets a laugh. The phrase "blow job" is harder to pin down as a homo-to-hetero term. It's been around for a long while—since 1942—and was an American phrase that eventually traveled to Britain. Etymologists disagree as to its origins. It could have come from the prostitute term "to blow someone off," meaning to release sexual energy, or from a nickname for very fast jet planes (blow jobs), or from jazz musician parlance of blowing an instrument. Homosexuals claimed "blow job" in the 1960s, around the time that Andy Warhol made his controversial film of the same name. The formerly vulgar term now seems to crop up everywhere, especially in casual heterosexual speech. Yet the first people I ever heard say it aloud were gay men, in the 1980s. "Blow job" seems to fall into that category of so many phrases—it has gone from straight to gay and then back to straight again.

Sexual terms that now stay firmly inside the gay community will continue to filter into straight conversation, especially terms for anal, oral, and manual sex, including rimming (oral/anal sex), teabagging (oral/scrotal sex), and fisting (hand-into-orifice sex). The concepts of "top" and "bottom" and "butch" and "femme" are just now making their way into the sexual vocabularies of hip straight people.

And while we're on the subject of the future of gay/straight language, I think that as gay men continue to assimilate, they will rehabilitate even more words to casually describe themselves. Just as "queer," a formerly pejorative term, has now been ennobled and is used freely by straight and gay people alike, we will see other former slurs emerge as safe and even prideful terms.

My bet for the next rehabilitated term is "faggot," which is already showing a major comeback in the gay community.

Chapter 3

Community,
Rituals,
and Home

Sometimes, the fact that a neighborhood is predominantly gay is the prime engine in increasing the value of its homes. Why? Gay homebuyers can be counted on to go beyond basic maintenance and cleaning of their properties, investing money, care and creativity in improving the properties. The result is a more attractive and desirable neighborhood that future homebuyers will be interested in.

—Robert Thomason, The Gay Financial Network

The [Black and White] ball was one of his major works. As much a major work as some of his short stories. He sat there planning it all summer long.

—Leo Lerman, talking about Truman Capote's famous
1966 party at the Plaza in New York City

It all began as a simple gathering of friends in 1984. Now, Halloween in New Orleans has evolved into one of the most celebrated gay circuit weekends of the year, and it is THE gay destination for Halloween.

—from a New Orleans tourist brochure

Home is where the heart is. If it is a stereotype that gay men like to make things look nice, is that so bad? All across the country, gay men renovate historical housing stock, creating enclaves for themselves and for artists of all sexual persuasions. Where they live, and the style in which they do it, is a great part of the heart of gay culture. Eventually, straight people flock to these places that have become so hip and lively.

Welcome to the "gayborhood."

The Village and Chelsea in New York, Provincetown, The Castro in San Francisco, Boys Town in Chicago, Germantown and Clintonville in Columbus, Ohio, Oaklawn in Dallas, Montrose in Houston, Capitol Hill in Seattle, Dupont Circle in Washington, D.C., South Beach in Miami—these and many other communities across the nation are setting the standard for trendy, hip places to live. With cafés, restaurants, and small, enticing shops, these places are on the vanguard of what people want in a community.

A friend just bought a house in Jersey City, New Jersey. Her husband was nervous on closing day until he met their future neighbors, a gay male couple gutting the structure next door, with plans for a total renovation.

"We're okay now," her husband said. "I know the neighborhood will improve. There are gay guys here."

Pioneers of the New Urban Civilization: Gays as First Movers

Until recently, proving the gay role in the revitalization of neighborhoods has been difficult, because most of the evidence has been anecdotal. In 1990, the U.S. government began counting gay citizens by group, and data have been emerging.

Demographer Gary Gates of the Urban Institute in Washington has been tracking the movement of the gay population, especially gay couples, for a few years. It's true, he told me, that gay men have a different attitude toward urban living and gentrification than do straight folks, and that gay men often lead the way into neighborhoods.

"One of the phenomena," says Gates, "is that gay men are concentrated in cities. For lack of another way of putting it, gay men tend to live in beautiful places. Why do gay men live in beautiful places with great amenities, such as San Francisco, New York, or Seattle? The short answer is: because they can."

Despite the recent gay interest in adopting children and raising families, says Gates, "gay men have tended to have a harder time having children. The costs for gay men to have children are higher than for heterosexuals, and the obstacles are higher, too."

So gay men have been able to divert their resources differently. The amount of disposable income homosexuals have has led to the myth that they make more money than heterosexual men, or that gay couples make more money than heterosexual couples. Not true, says Gates. "They earn less than other men, much less than married men—twelve percent less. Individual gay men are not innately prosperous—education levels are much higher, yet earnings are lower than married men."

However, when two men "couple," as Gates puts it, they can often afford more than a heterosexual couple. If gay men live outside the city, they usually live in expensive zip codes. The more expensive a place, the more likely it is to have higher concentrations of gay men—high costs in suburban locations are a better predictor than any other factor for a sizable gay population.

But what about the concentration of gays in cities? Gates and other demographers have data to support what everyone has known for a long time: Gay housing pioneers go to the worst places and then gentrify.

"Of any other coupling types, gay men live in places that have the highest levels of crime, oldest homes, and the highest-rising property values," says Gates, who has recently published a *Gay and Lesbian Atlas*. "All three of these factors suggest that gay men are 'first movers' into distressed neighborhoods."

Gates used the demographic term "first movers" to describe gay men in several categories. "First movers" are risk-takers who drive societal trends. For example, gay male couples are much more likely to be interracial or interethnic than straight couples, who are much more homogeneous. "It makes sense," says Gates. "Gays are willing to move into edgy areas, and also, because the homosexual marriage pool is limited, they are willing to take a chance on a person from a different background."

Well, if all this was starting to sound like utopia to me— gay couples gentrifying bad neighborhoods and living in interracial harmony—then what I learned next was going to clinch it for sure.

Yes, the homosexuals did really save civilization, because Gates and another researcher have discerned that a high gay population is necessary for a city's technological savvy and creative output.

In a study, "Technology and Tolerance," Gates and Richard Florida, a professor from Carnegie Mellon University in Pittsburgh, put forward an even bolder thesis about the benefits of having homos in the neighborhood. "The leading indicator of a metropolitan area's high-technology success," they wrote, "is a large gay population." They went on to name the top five high-technology areas—San Francisco, Washington, D.C., Austin, Atlanta, and San Diego—all of which have high gay populations. "Gays not only predict the concentration of high-tech industry, they are also a predictor of its growth."

Wow. Gay men are saving civilization, in a very high-tech way.

What's more, it seems that Richard Florida, in his research, has been trying to figure out what attracts young heterosexuals to particular jobs and communities. Surprise! It's gayness and rainbow flags!

In focus groups, Professor Florida found that brainy young college graduates were looking for tolerant and diverse neighborhoods near the companies that wanted to hire them. A test, it seemed, was if there were rainbow flags hanging in windows. They saw such flags as a sign of openness and tolerance. And even if they were straight, they judged their future workplaces by their policies toward benefits for gay couples and domestic partners.

The Diaspora, Housing Values, and How Long Can a Neighborhood Stay Gay?

West Hollywood, California, the town next to mine, is a very strange place. It's the gayborhood meets the shtetl. The town has a gay mayor and gay council members, but more than eight-thousand Russian immigrants also make "WeHo" home. The aging Russian-Jewish population coexists fairly well with the buff, young WeHo immigrants, whose average age seems to be twenty-five, but of course I'm imagining that second part. There are lots of apartment buildings that house the impossibly pretty young party boys. But there *are* older gay couples who stayed in WeHo after they bought into the real estate market in the 1990s.

In a 1999 interview with a real estate website, Josh Levin, a West Hollywood financial planner, described an area known as Norma Triangle, near Santa Monica Boulevard, where gay men had totally renovated the bungalows. "These are little homes built in the 1920s for railroad workers," he says. "We say the neighborhood has been 'fairy-dusted.' There is not a street with homes that gays haven't redesigned."

But, as is happening all over the country, West Hollywood has become pricey. Those fairy-dusted starter homes are not within reach of young gay people, and so they are leaving for other neighborhoods, such as Silver Lake or Downtown Los Angeles. The dream of the gay ghetto is disappearing, in part because of assimilation, and in larger part because straight people are moving in and driving up the prices even further.

The staff of *The Stranger,* an alternative newspaper in Seattle, lashed out at this phenomenon in 1999:

*The closest most gays and lesbians ever come to finding a promised land is moving to the gay ghetto—an urban neighborhood that is populated by, and reasonably tolerates, a large number of queers. Young, straight singles have moved in, followed by straight retirees, marrieds, and young families. With young queers forced to look elsewhere for housing, first-wave gay ghettos are on the decline, sapped of the energy and sex appeal of queer youngsters. Such is the sad story of Seattle's Capitol Hill ...
And thus the great queer migration begins. Queers set out, like herds of faaabulous caribou, in search of the next gay ghetto. It happened in New York, it happened in*

*Chicago, it happened in San Francisco—and now it's
happening here. All over the United States, young gays
and lesbians priced out of established gay ghettos are
colonizing new neighborhoods, seeking out cheap rents
and opening trendy restaurants. In New York, young
queers have abandoned the East Village and taken over
Chelsea; in Chicago, young queers have left Lake View
behind and taken over Andersonville, and in San Francisco, young queers have burst out of the Castro and
taken over, well, everything.*

And so the housing cycle is complete: Instead of just visit-
ing gay neighborhoods, straight people want to live in them.
Heterosexuals are like strange conquerors, wandering into an
ideal civilization built for them and abandoned by the indige-
nous population. Nice card shops, nice bars, great coffee
shops, interesting bookshops. Yes, gay neighborhoods are
what any civilized person would want.

The Definition of a Community:
It's Got to Have a Bingo Night!

Conceived as a fund-raiser for AIDS organizations in 1993,
Gay Bingo night in Seattle raises as much as $10,000 per night.
It's the perfect example of how the gay community can take a
rather boring heterosexual standby and make it into vital,
funny performance art. Seattle's Gay Bingo is so popular that
tickets sell out a week in advance, and it has spread to other

cities, such as Dallas, Philadelphia, Atlanta, Washington, D.C., Pittsburgh, and Cranston, Rhode Island. The Philadelphia public television station, WHYY, made a great documentary detailing a year in the Gay Bingo life. Since it started in Philadelphia in 1996, it has become a popular date night for heterosexuals, too.

The ingredients of Gay Bingo remain the same from town to town. First, there is always a drag-queen host. In Seattle right now, it's Glamazonia, played by Thom Hubert. In Philadelphia, until they quit in a huff two years ago, it was the famous gay duo Carlota Ttendant (Michael) and Chumley Singer, a divinely zany pair. The bingo night usually has a theme, like *The Wizard of Oz, Gilligan's Island, Singin' in the Rain,* or *Hawaii Five-O.* Tasteless jokes are made throughout the evening.

In Philadelphia, the Saturday-night bingo game features "a cheesy prom set," as its promoters boast. Much time is given over to ribald back-and-forth, such as Carlota Ttendent's confessions about having crushes on the Amish boys who work at sausage stands at the farmer's market.

In Seattle, the connection between the Catholic Church and bingo is emphasized by the administrations of the Sisters of Perpetual Indulgence, bearded transvestite nuns. And Glamazonia tries to do "dirty fast talking" to confuse the sign-language interpreters.

All bingo games have borrowed the original Seattle concept of having "BVDs"—Bonafide Verification Divas—in drag outfits and roller skates, zipping around the players to determine if a bingo card is really complete.

The real surprise has been what a draw Gay Bingo is for the

straight community. "This isn't your grandma's bingo game" is often the slogan. At some games, more than half the audience is straight. While some heterosexuals come because they've lost loved ones to AIDS and want to support a good cause, others just enjoy a good time.

The Seattle Times reported that some straight couples bring their children along. "The kids love it," said Dee Steele, forty-six, of Edmonds, Washington, whose kids are ages seven and ten. "Most of the jokes are over their heads, and it's not anything that's harmful. . . . This is a lot more fun than staying home and watching a movie."

Once again, gay men have taken a dull ritual associated with little old ladies in church basements and made it hip and fun. When I first joined my outdoor pool club in Philadelphia in 1986, the tradition of the Saturday-night bingo game held on but was poorly attended. That was when club membership was comprised mostly of elderly people and young straight couples with kids. I never went to the upper deck to play—it was too depressing just hearing the constant drone of the bingo announcer wafting out over the water. In the nineties, many gay men moved into my neighborhood, and the number of queer swimmers increased by 30 percent. As soon as the homosexual population reached a critical mass, gay guys took over the dreary bingo night and made it campy fun, with silly prizes and routines. Almost immediately, bingo night became a standing-room-only affair at the Lombard Swim Club, with straights and gays merrily socializing. I hate bingo, and even I couldn't resist the shtick of the gay master of ceremonies.

Of course, at our small swim club's bingo night, all the

proceeds went to the winners. But the large Gay Bingo celebrations are always AIDS events. Raising money for people
living with HIV and its consequences is a skill so developed in
the gay community that straight charities have been trying to
emulate it for years. In Philadelphia, there is a lot of cross-
pollination between gay organizations and traditionally straight
organizations and events. For example, Chumley Singer, the
creator of Philadelphia's Gay Bingo, has also directed the
city's Fourth of July and New Year's Eve celebrations. He's
planned traditional Thanksgiving Day parade events as well
as events for PrideFest America.

Sing OUT, Young Man: Gay Choruses, Mixed Audiences

Gay Bingo, with its costumes and camp and exuberant tone,
exemplifies what gay guys do best: They take something simple and make it better. Gay singing groups are also in that
category.

American communities love to sing. There have always
been church choirs, high-school choruses, a cappella groups,
and barbershop quartets.

But America ain't seen nothin' like gay choruses!

They've changed attitudes toward amateur choral singing
while also, on occasion, adding the humor and camp that's
mostly missing from the straight choral scene. Since 1977,
when the first one, the Stonewall Chorale, appeared in New
York, gay choruses of all types have sprung up in urban

and suburban areas. The San Francisco Gay Men's Chorus (SFGMC) claims to be the first to use "gay" in its title—it started in 1978 as some singers gathered on the steps of City Hall to sing and mourn the assassination of Harvey Milk. By 2001, the SFGMC had performed at Carnegie Hall and the Kennedy Center.

The Gay Men's Chorus of Los Angeles, now in its twenty-fifth season, has crossed over to the straight world by appearing on an episode of *Will & Grace* (costarring Matt Damon as a straight guy who wants to join so that he can get a free trip to Europe), and on an entire season of *Six Feet Under*. (Michael, the gay brother, auditioned and got into the chorus. He performed along with real chorus members.) They've toured the world, sung for former President Clinton, and performed with Bernadette Peters, Joanna Gleason, Angela Lansbury, Rita Moreno, Beatrice Arthur, and Jerry Herman. It's a far cry from singing at the town picnic.

The gay choral movement is growing by leaps and bounds, and entertaining at more mainstream events every year with many heterosexuals in attendance. There are groups that sing only Gregorian chants, groups that sing only classical music, and many others that mix genres including rock, jazz, and even commercial jingles. I've never seen anything funnier than a performance by a small gay chorus, The Spruce Street Singers in Philadelphia, which sang in serious, soulful tones the "I Wish I Were an Oscar Mayer Wiener" song. I would have liked to have attended the performance of Captain Smarty-pants, a small offshoot of the Seattle Men's Chorus, when it did an entire original song cycle, "Fruit of the Month Club."

I know a bit about the urban gay singing scene, but I was surprised to find groups that were based in smaller towns and some that were aimed at a statewide audience. Of all the hundreds of performance descriptions, I most preferred the details of two concerts by the Connecticut Gay Men's Chorus. They show how gay-tolerant small towns in Connecticut have become.

Queer Eye for the Magi (Christmas 2003)

Well, wouldn't you want a makeover if you'd just spent a thousand miles on a camel? Three newly fabulous kings join our merry men, eight dancing reindeer, some decidedly unusual elves, Santa, Martha Stewart and Joan Crawford in an evening that will tickle your fancy and roast your chestnuts.

Flaming Saddles (June 2004)

Journey with our Cos Cob cowboys to the dusty trails and big skies of the Old West, where men were men and accessories were very difficult to find. Yep. Silver spurs, rawhide chaps and rhinestone tiaras—they're all here. But along the way be prepared for a wild ride as the boys rassle with contemporary gender politics and hoedown with the Supreme Court.

I wish my high-school chorus had done theme concerts of that type, instead of making us sing old arrangements of tired old *Man of La Mancha* songs.

It's My Party and I'll Cry
If I Want To . . .

Want to have a great party? Ask a gay man to plan it. Celebration is an intense part of gay life; homosexual rituals have spilled over into heterosexual communities, making the tradition of American parties and gatherings more flamboyant than in past decades. There is, of course, even a stereotype of the gay party planner who tries to educate boring straight people, as exemplified by the characters Martin Short and B. D. Wong play in the *Father of the Bride* movies.

But some stereotypes are true. Many gay men are tireless when it comes to new and fresh ideas for entertaining.

My best friend threw herself a fortieth birthday party and hired a mutual friend, a gay man. He decided it should have a Moroccan theme, and when my friend said she had no Moroccan decorations, he blithely replied, "Hey, no problem, we'll tent the place!" And that's what he did, in her tiny apartment. He erected poles and draped Middle Eastern fabric everywhere. By the time he got finished, it looked like a seventeenth-century harem. The party was an enormous success, and a very gay touch was the fez her pet cat wore for the occasion.

In this celebrity-crazed world, party planners themselves have become famous, and so many of them are gay. When Oprah was planning her fiftieth birthday party at a mansion in Montecito, California, the television show *Extra* interviewed Colin Cowie, "gay party guru," as the interviewer called him. "To give a good party," said Cowie, "there are three great rules: great food, fabulous music, and tasty, snappy cocktails." If we didn't know it already, we'd catch on that Cowie is gay by the appearance of "fabulous" and "snappy" in the same sentence.

When columnist Michelangelo Signorile outed the recently deceased Malcolm Forbes in a cover story in *Outweek* in 1990, I was as surprised as most people. But then I thought, *Hey, but what about that seventieth birthday party Malcolm threw for himself under the desert stars in Morocco? What about those balloon rides over the French countryside with Fran Leibowitz? How about his deep and abiding friendship with Elizabeth Taylor?* All gay, gay, gay.

Gay men invented the party that people would travel for.

Cole Porter was famous for the bashes he gave at his rented palace in Venice. Truman Capote spent a year planning his 1966 Black and White Ball at the Plaza Hotel in New York for his guest of honor, Katharine Graham of *The Washington Post.* Capote was more hands-on than most party queens—he obsessed over everything, from invitations to color schemes, and spent a lot of his time coquettishly trying to prevent guest-list leaks. By the time his party was ready to go, the fun part was gone. As the San Francisco columnist Herb Caen told George Plimpton in an oral history of Capote, "[The Black and White Ball] was like the Super Bowl. There was such a buildup that by the time the game was played, it didn't amount to much."

Another writer, Peter Mathiessen, said that Truman Capote had always remained angry that he skipped the Black and White Ball because of a deadline. "When I asked if I was forgiven, he burst out, 'Cecil Beaton came all the way from London for my party, and you wouldn't even come in from Sagaponack!'"

According to many accounts, Capote's Black and White Ball was a turning point in American party history. Said Norman Podhoretz, "[T]he confluence of the fashionable social world, and the literary world and the world of political power was embodied in that guest list." In Capote, we see a gay man with a vision: He wanted to arrange famous people, and have them dance and sway to his own music. A highlight of the party was when Lauren Bacall danced with Jerome Robbins, the gay choreographer of *West Side Story* fame. Those who attended the Black and White Ball almost forty years ago are still talking about it.

Flash-forward ten years. Steve Rubell, the not-quite-out gay man who owned the infamous Studio 54 in New York with Ian Schrager, would also change the way Americans perceived a party. Opening in 1977, Studio 54 was instantly the most popular place to be seen with artists, authors, rock stars, models, and actors partying the night away underneath a big moon emblem featuring a moving cocaine spoon. Much has been written about the cultural effect of the disco world of the 1970s, and especially the gay sensibility that created the supermodel and the super-celebrity. In 1998, a pre–Austin Powers Mike Myers starred as Rubell in a flop of a movie, *54*.

Although Rubell was the co-owner of Studio 54 and presumably could have delegated doorman duties, he insisted that his presence at the entrance was the key to a good party mix. He was the ultimate gay host in that sense, fussing over every detail. "That's why I stay by the door," Rubell told Bob Colacello in *Interview* magazine in 1978. "People say, why do you subject yourself to staying at the door? But if I leave the door alone, the crowd doesn't end up the way I want it. There's a certain type of person we don't pass. People come to me and say, 'I'm a millionaire from Tucson, Arizona,' but I don't care if they're not fun . . ."

Rubell didn't like to admit large numbers of single women, because 54 was not a straight pickup bar.

"Is it a gay bar, basically?" asked Colacello.

"It's bisexual," said Rubell. "Very, very, very bisexual. And that's how we choose the crowd, too. In another words, we want everyone to be fun and good-looking."

Rubell, who later served a short jail term for tax evasion and died of AIDS in 1991, invented the blueprint for a new social life—an elitist yet utopian party where gays and straights mingled together in the constant quest to be hip. His influence can still be felt at the velvet ropes of exclusive clubs, and especially any place that celebrity is worshipped excessively, such as on the E! network or at awards events.

Although Studio 54 turned out to be fairly short-lived, the gay spirit of celebration lives on in different kinds of totally gay "black-and-white parties" held across the nation: circuit parties. Born in the late 1980s, circuit parties are a no-holds-barred hedonistic ritual of gay life. "Circuit boys," the young, buff, bedrugged participants in parties around the country, are a potent symbol of the gay lifestyle, which may or may not still exist. While circuit-party participants represent the joie de vivre of gay life, they also represent danger, drugs, and unsafe sex.

Not many employed or partnered gay men have the time or energy to follow the circuit, but each party in each city spotlights and reaffirms that the gay community is here to stay. Every circuit party presents a Mardi Gras situation—sort of like a homosexual version of spring break, or *Girls Gone Wild*, come to think of it. Large circuit parties include the Black Party in New York (in March), the Cherry series in Washington, D.C. (in May), the White Party in Palm Springs (April), the Black-and-Blue Ball in Montreal (October), and smaller events, like Fireball in Chicago (February), the Purple Party in Dallas (May), and Blue Ball in Philadelphia (January).

In past civilizations, regular citizens have always been given license to go insane during brief periods of time. Fastnacht in Germany, for example, was supposed to be a time when husbands and wives could get drunk, escape from each other, and possibly even have a sexual encounter with someone outside their marriage. The only vestige of such events today exists in the gay community, which shows how much we straight people need such arenas. I predict that these gay-specific events will leave their mark on heterosexual populations, as other gay party rituals have.

Halloween: The New Gay Holiday, and Going Straighter Every Year

Halloween has been called the gay Christmas. But the actual gay Christmas is fun enough—why not just examine the enormous influence the gay population has had on how we celebrate Halloween itself?

Halloween has a long, storied, pagan past that has nothing to do with its current commercial appeal, of course. But in the 1960s, 1970s, and even well into the 1980s, the holiday was completely juvenilized. Halloween was by kids, for kids, and about kids. I remember, in the late 1960s, that my father was the only adult who put on a costume in our suburban neighborhood.

Then the tide began to change. First came the many trick-or-treating food scares, which started to force Halloween off the streets and into homes and party halls. Then, in the late 1980s, Halloween merchandise began to appear as early as back-to-school time, before Labor Day. Some people have traced the new adult fascination with Halloween to an inability to mature. Baby boomers wanted to have as much fun as their children. But does this explain why Halloween suddenly shot up the charts, becoming a legitimate adult holiday with sales revenues second only to Christmas sales?

Changing baby boomer attitudes probably had something to do with a surge in the grown-up dollars given over to the holiday, but I also don't think we can underestimate the gay influence. In the last twenty years, in cities all across the nation, Halloween has become larger than life through gay parades and celebrations. And as the years go on, straight people are looking more toward the gay community to define a Halloween celebration.

As early as 1995, straight revelers outnumbered gay participants at the Halloween parade in San Francisco's Castro district. The parade had started as an event for neighborhood children in the 1980s, but then transformed into a gay event as the Castro became, essentially, a gay ghetto. Farther south in California, in the gay enclave of West Hollywood, a parade had also started in the mid-eighties. According to West Hollywood's official website, in 2001, 55 percent of parade attendees were straight, 37 percent were gay, and 8 percent were lesbian.

Gay and straight people are mingling at Halloween events all across the country; many Halloween events are becoming destination events, attracting heterosexuals as well as homosexuals. Peter Tatchell, writing in the travel section of the British paper *The Guardian* in 2001, gave the thumbs-up to the annual Fantasy Fest, a weeklong carnival that takes place in Key West, Florida.

Middle America can go jump in the Atlantic (it's at the end of the main street). A third of the town's population is gay, and liberal values reign supreme. Although Fantasy Fest is not a gay event, the gay influence is everywhere. Queers know how to party and heterosexuals are grateful for an invitation. Families mix happily with dykes and fags. This is the world how it should be—love and let love.

If gay men have claimed and reinvented the all-American Halloween, can Christmas be far behind? In the New York City Macy's Thanksgiving Day Parade in 2003, the crowd saw two Santa Claus figures: the "real" Santa Claus, who always rides at the end of the parade, and "Mrs. Santa Claus," played in drag by Harvey Fierstein. When Fierstein wrote an op-ed piece in *The New York Times*, saying that Mrs. Claus was part of a same-sex marriage, public-relations chaos ensued. Macy's stressed that Mrs. Claus was not really being being played by a gay man, but rather by Harvey's female character, Edna Turnblad, the star of the Broadway show *Hairspray*—a strange distinction. The Macy's spokesperson also noted that Fierstein's Mrs. Claus was in no way meant to be a substitute for Santa Claus. Clearly, though, we were seeing gay inroads being made into mainstream Christmas traditions.

He's Dead, but We Can Still Have a Party: Gay Advances in Mourning Rituals

In Richard Curtis's romantic comedy *Four Weddings and a Funeral* (1994), a gay character, Matthew, chooses to read W. H. Auden's intense poem, "Funeral Blues," in honor of his lover at his funeral: "He was my North, my South, my East and West./ My working week and my Sunday rest . . ." The inclusion of the poem in the film led to renewed fascination with the gay poet Auden's work. Small editions of the work were republished in Great Britain and the United States. Mostly, I think that people were captivated by the romantic sentiment of the work. Rarely, before 1988 or so, were people accustomed to hearing impassioned readings or funeral speeches. Funerals were not very unique occasions. But the death of so many young gay men in the 1980s changed our funeral customs. For the first time since World War I, vast numbers of gay and straight people had to come to terms with early death.

When someone dies in the prime of life, it is easy to memorialize his more flamboyant traits. I recall one man who died of AIDS in Philadelphia; he had been in city government, and had also been a fanatic fan of the Mummers, the city's unique befeathered string bands. His funeral featured a squad of Mummers bursting into the church, playing "Oh Dem Golden Slippers" on banjos, fiddles, and guitars. Since no one had been able to agree about who would dispose of the deceased's ashes, the funeral party adjourned to a boat on the Delaware River, where attendees were each given a small plastic bag of the dead man's ashes, festooned with sequins. And so, bit by bit, their friend was disposed of as they drank cocktails and watched the sunset.

It's interesting that one of the most popular television shows on today, *Six Feet Under*, was created by a gay man and features a funeral home run by a gay man and his straight brother. One episode featured the request of a gay mourner to mount a scene from an opera at his lover's funeral. Although it is difficult to prove, I would argue that the gay community's response to AIDS deaths has influenced mainstream America's attitude toward the memorial service. Above all, gay funerals are coming out of a new tradition of individuality, and the idea that friends are as important as family and deserve to be part of memorials. As is the case with most trends, straight mourners are beginning to adopt these new practices. In the future, the flair and uniqueness seen in many gay funerals will also become a part of heterosexual rituals.

Book Two

Body

Chapter 4

Eat Me: Gay Dishes, Straight Appetites, Common Thirsts

It follows that all food *pretending* to be something else is food in drag.

—David Mehnert, *Slate* magazine

Brunch is a gastronomic bandage, a meal designed to carry middle-aged homosexuals and other disappointed people through the nameless terrors of the weekend and, generally, into a resigned, more starchy future. The food is less important than the tone of the experience, because brunch is a consolation meal and should be served as if offered at one's sickbed. It's the least a handsome waiter can do.

—R. M. Vaughan

U Stareho Songu, Prague's first queer restaurant, is a kitshy, roomy space . . . serving traditional Czech cuisine rechristened with delightfully campy names.

—from a gay travel guide to Eastern Europe

A brief look at Bruce Feirstein's 1982 hyper-masculine humor book, *Real Men Don't Eat Quiche*, shows how threatened straight people once were by homosexual tendencies related to food, and how far we've come. Quiche once seemed a bit exotic and a little gay—now it's served in airport restaurants.

Food lacks specific connotation until prepared, and there's no doubt that food cooked and served by gay men has a certain flair, or sensibility. Nouvelle cuisine was invented by mostly heterosexual French chefs in the early 1970s. It featured reduced amounts of fat and butter, miniscule portions of fish and meat, and strange sauces made with fresh herbs. Its greatest proponent was Craig Claiborne, the openly gay food columnist for *The New York Times* from 1957 to 1986.

Claiborne's influence is still felt in kitchens everywhere. His *New York Times Cookbook*, first published in 1961, sold three million copies, and he was generally acknowledged to be America's most well-known food writer throughout the 1960s and 1970s. Born in 1920 in Mississippi, he was a gracious "man's man" who served in the navy during World War II and then again during the Korean War, after he had trained as a chef in France. Claiborne never really had a steady homosexual relationship. Yet he firmly remained a part of New York gay society while also influencing heterosexual family cooks throughout the country. He was the first of the early food writers to experiment with health trends, such as low-sodium foods, and to bring a new, more delicate way of eating to the general public. America learned about fresh herbs from Craig Claiborne long before Alice Waters and Jeremiah Tower and the whole California-cuisine revolution started.

It's hard to exactly define queer food and drink. But I've certainly encountered them. In the early 1990s, I was a member of a Shakespeare reading group. Every month we would meet to read a play and have dinner, switching from house to house. There were two single gay men in the group; the others were single women or heterosexual couples. On their assigned nights, the heterosexuals made respectable repasts designed for casual gatherings: chili, pasta, casseroles.

On the night we read *Macbeth*, though, we were in for a veritable feast of gay-inspired food. The gay man preparing the meal had put hours of thought into the menu, which was totally inspired by the play. We had roast lamb marinated in mead (honey-wine) vinegar and stewed with turnips, a meal that could have been enjoyed by Macbeth and his lady. The side dish was Scottish oatmeal roasted with onions and nuts. It was the first time I'd had oatmeal served as a side dish. It was delicious, and totally appropriate for our reading. Our host had even gone so far as to put a dagger on the table as a centerpiece.

I think it's one of the gayest meals I've ever had. It was perfect in content and tone, and planned down to the nth detail. It made our reading of *Macbeth* special, and I recall that it was the only time we'd gotten through a whole Shakespearean tragedy in one night.

What Makes a Meal Gay, and How Can I Tell If I Am in a Gay Restaurant?

Gay food features exotic ingredients and flamboyant presentations. Long before "fusion" became a popular food term, gays were fusing the dramatic and culinary arts. I first heard the term "napped," used to describe a sauce, from one of my gay friends. (This means a sauce placed on the bottom of a plate.)

It's hard to remember how gay men were pioneers of gourmet food, because upscale food items are now so accessible to middle America.

Many of the more exotic ingredients now available everywhere in supermarkets were long staples in gay kitchens and restaurants, including pesto, hummus, olive tapenade, balsamic vinegar, quinoa, grapeseed oil, mesclun, sushi, caviar, wild mushrooms, and arborio rice.

As always happens in the gay circle game, whenever something gets too popular or at least too familiar, gay chefs and diners turn to new places for culinary inspiration. Gay chefs were some of the first to notice the backlash against nouvelle cuisine and begin offering heartier fare. I first started seeing what I call Retro-Camp Cuisine at gay restaurants about ten years ago. Gay men were the first to revamp comfort food and add exciting dashes of flair. They took the home cooking of their youths and elevated it.

Many restaurants in gay neighborhoods now offer stuff that at first sounds very *Leave It to Beaver*–ish. They might have a meat loaf with mashed potatoes–type dish on the menu, yet often the meat loaf is made with veal and the potatoes are mashed with morels or wasabi. Fifties classics such as macaroni and cheese, french fries, pork chops, and hamburgers all take on new guises in a gay restaurant. I ordered Buffalo wings at a gay diner in Washington, D.C.—they came with fried leeks instead of celery. And I washed it all down with a great cosmopolitan.

I always used to recommend checking out gay travel sites in order to make sure that you can find civilized restaurants at your destination. In addition to being civilized, they'll usually be more fun. Check out the comments about the gay quotient of a London café, from reviewer Adrian Gillin of the zine *Out UK*.

Lobster Pot is one of the gayest finds in town. You step in off a grimy Lambeth street to a marine experience and I mean "Hello sailor," full-on Jean Paul Gaultier. With fish swimming around in port-holes and loos echoing to the sound of seagulls, you'll be one of but a dozen guests served up fresh fish, in or out of shell, in this snug culinary cabin—a treat.

Or how about this entrée description in a menu from a gay resort, Turtle Cove, on the Australian coast: "Peppered kangaroo rump sliced over a roast capsicum risotto and topped with pureed roast eggplant."

How a Homosexual Invented Straight Barbecue and Deviled Eggs

What could be straighter than the tradition of the outdoor barbecue? Male participation in cookouts became very popular after the Second World War. The growth of the suburbs created the lawns that spawned the outdoor grills and encouraged male cooks, right? Male interest in the grill seems a natural result of demographics and geography.

Well, not exactly.

It took a *gay* man, the famous food writer and chef James Beard, to get husbands everywhere off the couch and into aprons. Beard wrote the first articles and the standard cookbook on barbecuing. He made it acceptable for heterosexual guys to cook outdoors.

"Men who wouldn't think of touching a switch on an electric stove, much less of preparing a meal thereon, suddenly discover a gift for preparing the proper bed of coals in a grill," Beard wrote in *House & Garden* in 1956. "Others suddenly reveal a genius for cooking meat to a turn." Ironically, Beard made outdoor cooking less "sissy" for the straight men of America.

Beard, like Craig Claiborne, became a gay cooking icon, even though, also like Claiborne, he seems to have had a fairly unhappy life as a gay man. Born in Portland, Oregon, in 1903, Beard had tried to make a living as an actor and an opera singer in his youth until he found his true niche, parlaying his mother's training in food preparation into a career as a chef and cookbook author. He was among the first to trumpet regional cuisine and down-home American cooking. He excelled at the grill and in the fine task of making unusual appetizers for cocktail parties. One of his specialties was simple but incredibly delicious deviled eggs, which he adapted from the South and then introduced into the hors d'oeuvres canon in the 1950s (which is ironic, since deviled eggs are usually considered the ultimate straight picnic or church supper food).

The butchy Beard really pushed the masculine outdoor grill prerogative, saying in his earliest grilling book, "We believe [charcoal cookery] is primarily a man's job and that a woman, if she's smart, will keep it that way." This irked his coauthor, Helen Evans Brown. According to Robert Clark, in *The Solace of Food: A Life of James Beard*, "Helen would often say to James, 'As usual, the boys win.'"

The Drag-Queen Chef and Icon: Miss Julia

To some gay men, the gayest food person they ever saw was a straight female chef, the very tall and strangely voiced Julia

Child. "Julia is really just a big drag queen," says Nelson Aspen, forty, author of *Let's Have a Gay Dinner Party!* and *Let's Dish Up a Dinner Party*.

"Julia is so camp, she even looks like a drag queen, which is wonderful. She could give RuPaul a run for his money any day. I mean, how could we gay boys not be attracted to cooking, growing up with Julia and Graham [Kerr] on television?" Aspen acknowledges that Australian cooking celebrity Graham Kerr was not gay, but says he was certainly gay-friendly, and flamboyant in his over-the-top cooking demonstrations as the Galloping Gourmet.

"With both of them, you felt as if they were winking at you from the TV set, welcoming you into their world," says Aspen, who escaped into that world as a fat, gay little kid. His own cookbooks are incredible displays of the gay food aesthetic—comforting recipes with kitschy titles like Nelson's Big Succulent Coq au Vin, A Star is Born Caviar (caviar atop beet and jicama slices made with a star-shaped cookie cutter), Chicken? Dump Him, Darling!, and The Lord Is My Shepherd's Pie.

Julia was the Martha Stewart of her time, bringing the foreign flair of French cooking into America's homes. (One *Toronto Sun* article in 1995 saw it the other way around, saying that Martha Stewart is the Julia Child of cocooning, or household decoration.)

Many baby boomers remember Julia not so much from her famous PBS cooking show in the 1960s and 1970s, or from her many cookbooks, but rather from the hilarious *Saturday Night Live* sketch in which Dan Aykroyd does an unusual turn of drag. Aykroyd, in a bad wig, dress, and tacky apron, camps it up, cutting himself with a sharp knife and then slowly bleeding to death because the phone in the studio kitchen is fake. He mimics Julia's high, mincing voice, and as he slumps to the floor, he advises viewers to "save the liver" of the chicken for future culinary use. Julie Powell, who recently completed a blog project of cooking all Julia Child's recipes, admits that it is this high-drag version of Julia that most impressed her when she was growing up: "Julia Child was, to me, Dan Aykroyd in an apron gushing blood. . . ."

In the pre–Food Network world, Julia Child was a constant reference in identifying gay "foodies" in the 1970s. Says one fan website of Paul Lynde, "[Most] of the articles about Paul from the 1970s dealt with his palatial Hollywood mansions or his inner Julia Child."

The Cocktail Circle of Life

In the early 1990s, gay men reinvented the vintage drinks that were so much a part of the Waspy country-club scene after World War II. Straight people should be eternally grateful for being rescued from the drab 1980s days of the white-wine spritzers and rotgut Chardonnay served in tacky fern bars.

Gay men led the way to the $10 sipping cocktail with extravagant accoutrements. The cosmopolitan, the martini, the Manhattan, and more have all been gussied up with new ingredients so that they barely resemble the mixed drinks our parents loved. Along with the cocktails come the fabulous hors d'oeuvres—finger foods of the gods. Cocktail weenies are back, and mostly because gay hors d'oeuvres chefs put them out again. Yet gay cocktail weenies are always better, somehow. (Okay, hold the double entendres!) I have a friend who makes them out of the finest little dogs he can buy, and of course with a dash of irony. He brings them to every party he attends. He does them as pigs in blankets, but the "blanket" part is made out of puff pastry, not regular dough.

Cosmopolitans, especially, have made it into every mainstream bar in America. The girls on *Sex and the City* used to drink them until they became so common that they're no longer hip. Now the Manhattan is edging out the cosmo, and straight people are experimenting with exotic flavored martinis, once very gay and now a fixture on the straight single bar scene.

A word here must be said about vodka, nectar of the gay gods. Gay men were in the forefront of the clear-liquor revolution, changing America from a "scotch on the rocks" country to a vodka martini kind of place. Absolut, which targeted gay consumers as early as the mid-eighties, has long been the gay vodka of choice. In its clever ads, Absolut began incorporating the work of gay artists such as Keith Haring, and the brand also participated in fashion promotional events, which increased its visibility in the gay community. Within a few years it was the number-one vodka in the gay market, and then became number one in the entire country.

The Future of Gay Cocktail Culture: Sex on the Beach for Everyone!

It was New Year's Eve, 1989. I was eight months pregnant and in a predominantly gay restaurant. Alas, I could not drink. But after midnight had come, droves of half-naked men wandered around in a conga line, screaming "Sex on the beach! Who wants sex on the beach? Let's have sex on the beach!" Of course, they were talking about the drink Sex on the Beach. But I'd never heard of it before. Although I can't prove that the drink's origins were gay, it was a few years more before I saw Sex on the Beach available at straight bars. It's very difficult to pin down a drink's history, but I did see one reference to Sex on the Beach on a straight, hyper-heterosexual bar menu listed as new, "the hottest drink of Summer 1999." That was a good ten years after I first heard about it in gay venues.

A few years ago, gay friends told me about the Black Bitch, a drink made with Coke and vodka. What amused me most, though, was the Skinny Black Bitch, made with Diet Coke. Now those drinks are available in straight bars, as well as The Screaming Orgasm, an orangey, creamy concoction that has crossed over to the heterosexual cocktail world.

Of course, there are other descriptively named drinks served at gay bars throughout the country that are probably at least another decade away from making the transition to straight cocktails. The Anal Penetrator, for example, or the Anal Probe. I'm voting for Liquid Pants Remover (LPR) to make the jump from homo to hetero bars soon.

"What makes a drink 'gay'?" asked David Schmader in Seattle's alternative newspaper, *The Stranger*. "Some say all it takes is a name ending in 'rita' or 'tini,' while others specify the inclusion of chopped fruit and fanciful decorations." Schmader wrote a hilarious piece in which he took a straight friend around to gay bars to see if drinking "frou-frou" drinks would make him gay.

> *The subject's first "gay drink" of the night was a Grape Nehi (2 oz vodka, 2 oz raspberry liqueur, lemon, blended with ice), given an extra splash of gay by our accommodating bartender, who crowned the drink with a spear of maraschino cherries and a paper umbrella. . . . Next we came to the stylish dance club Blu, where the friendly boy-tender answered my call for "the gayest drink in the house" by whipping up an Aquapolitan (3 oz orange-lemon aquavit, 1 oz Grand Marnier, dash of orange juice, splash of cranberry juice/sour mix), which the subject described as "good" and "slushy."*

After also pouring a Cabana Boy Sunset and several cosmopolitans down his friend's throat, reporter Schmader concludes that a night of gay drinking makes a straight guy more loquacious, but not particularly gay.

"Ultimately," Schmader observes, "gay drinks are like big, fruity hugs—warming you up, raising your self-esteem, and going down easy." That's probably why so many straight people like to drink them, too.

Chapter 5

Fashion, Style, and Body Image: Gay Guys Do It Better!

Gay guys are the fashion designers of their own bodies, and then they just put tight things on top.

> —Mathieu Chantelois, host of the
> Canadian cable show *SoGayTv*

Karen: Jack, I've spent years and my husband's millions learning about fashion. What are your qualifications?

Jack: I'm gay.

Karen: Oh, honey, what would I do without you?

> —from an episode of *Will & Grace*

While I applaud the fierce courage that it must take to show up in public wearing clothing designed by hetero-sexuals, I don't think I will be able to walk a mile in your shoes—much less in the unsightly gowns you will be left to choose from.

> —from Mrs. Betty Bowers, America's Best Christian,
> explaining why she still picks homosexual
> designers, even if they are going to hell

If I hadn't been a woman, I'd have been a drag queen.

> —Dolly Parton

Is it just a stereotype that gay men are inherently fashionable? That they look and smell better than heterosexual guys? That they care more about their bodies, their furniture, and their wall coverings?

Maybe, but does it matter? Sometimes the most positive stereotypes are true.

"The notion that gay men have a superior fashion sense is not true, and it's damaging," openly gay Massachusetts Congressman Barney Frank told *Newsweek*. He finds the makeover show *Queer Eye for the Straight Guy* "offensive," because it creates the impression that gay men only care about decorating and style issues.

Lighten up, Barney. Of course not every gay man has great style. You don't, Barney, and some of my friends admit that they don't. ("I'm gay, but I dress like a fourteen-year-old boy from Indiana," says one gay man I know.) But shouldn't we be grateful for the growing public perception of queers as style mavens? Is it so bad to deal with a positive stereotype?

Beneath this stereotype lies a long history of how gay fashion attitudes have influenced the straight world.

The older, less subtle stereotype about gays and fashion was that they controlled it. I remember as a little kid, in the mid-sixties, hearing a mean person say that the "faggots" who designed women's couture didn't care if women looked awful in it. They were all flaming homosexuals who hated girls and wanted them to look bad in outré dresses. How stupidly homophobic can a person be?

Of course fashion has a very gay history. In fact, it could be argued that the essence of fashion is gay. Gay designers have influenced every straight woman's fashion choices for the last hundred years. It has always been a complicated gender issue: Gay designers create the looks deemed "sexy" to heterosexual audiences. Bill Blass, Christian Dior, Perry Ellis, Tom Ford, Fred Halston, Karl Lagerfeld, Helmut Lang, Christian La Croix, Isaac Mizrahi, Yves Saint Laurent, and Gaultier are only a few of the many homosexuals who have left an imprint on the fashion world. Gay men even invented the supermodel for straight men to drool over.

But as much as gay men influenced the tastes of wealthy women and definitely put the skinny, boyish silhouette on a pedestal (or runway), their influence goes far deeper than haute couture. When it comes to wardrobes, there has been, as in other areas, that same gay-to-straight "circle of life" that has affected what straight people wear and how they think about their bodies.

The steady transfer of fads and trends from gay to straight closets has been going on since the 1950s and 1960s, and has accelerated in the post-Stonewall era. America's newfound affection for the talents of gay stylists is merely a delayed reaction to a fait accompli. All of a sudden, heterosexuals have awakened to the huge influence gay men have had on our everyday fashion preferences.

Straight Men Who Look Gay: The Fashion Circle

Many of the trendy fashion looks for today's straight man had their origins in gay communities. Gay men even invented the "manly" look of today.

In the late 1970s, gay men in the Castro district of San Francisco rebelled against the stereotype of the effeminate homosexual and began wearing an ultra-masculine uniform of Levi's 501 jeans and flannel shirts. Sporting short hair and mustaches, they became known as "Castro Clones." The clone haircut and tight-jean look became trendy for straight guys about a decade later. When the Castro Clone look modified itself, throwing away the flannel shirts and embracing form-fitting T-shirts and polos, straight fashion eventually followed.

Straight male hairstyles always follow homosexual trends, too, and at an amazing speed. When gay haircuts became even more closely cropped, straight men followed suit only a few years later. Right now many fashionable straight men are wearing their hair closely clipped or shaved off entirely. (Consider the trendy pates of heterosexuals Daniel Day Lewis, Bruce Willis, Howie Mandel, Adam Sandler, and Matt Lauer.)

Hank Stuever, a *Washington Post* style writer, explained the origin of the gay haircut thing in the pages of Seattle's alternative newspaper *The Stranger*:

> *About 10 years ago, when there was a culture war for gay rights going on, the men of my generation went down and enlisted. We signed up for the Caesar 'do and Navy recruit buzz, which drifted into the George Clooney and Gap Zombie looks. Some MEN went shorter, then shorter, then just shaved their heads. We bought expensive Aveda gels and plastered our short hair to our heads, making it stick up just a tad in front. The next generation will look at pictures of us waving protest signs at Christian Coalition conventions and wonder which ones were the rabid conservatives and which ones were the radical activists.*

The gay-to-straight trickle-down fashion process has happened with tattoos, leather pants and jackets, and, of course, earrings. How would straight men know what to wear if gay guys hadn't worn it first? One of my friends bought her husband a leather jacket for Christmas, and then took him to her homosexual hairstylist for a cut. Her husband, catching a glimpse of himself in the mirror, said, "Could I look any gayer?"

A few other heavily gay-influenced fashion items and trends:

Shoes: How do gay men know, almost automatically, how to change footwear? The Castro Clone look always featured boots, but then gradually, even gay men began to wear cool running shoes. But about five years ago, suddenly every gay man I knew was wearing nicer, lighter hiking boots, and straight men followed soon afterward. And flip-flops. Except for surfers, the only men who wore them were gay. Now straight guys wear them all the time, too.

T-shirts: Gay men started the trend of the tight, form-fitting T-shirt. And also the infamous "wife beater" (a white, ribbed undershirt, so called because it refers to men who hang around the house in their underwear, waiting to get belligerent and beat their wives—*blecch*). As far as T-shirts and muscle shirts go, it's often hard to tell a young straight man and a young gay man apart. There's even a game, Gay or Guido?, that has been around for a while and was the inspiration for a monthly feature in *Details* magazine. The simple rules: Try to guess if the young guys in the wife beaters are homosexual or just young, straight Italian studs. (Now there's a whole website devoted to pictures of such guys.)

Jeans and Pants: Hippies brought denim pants into mainstream America's closets, but gay guys have defined how they're worn, from the designer jeans of the eighties to the manly Levi's 501s of the nineties and beyond. The fairly new "ripped look" started in gay circles—five years ago, young gay men in Hollywood (admittedly wasted young men) wandered around with holes in their knees and even in the seats of their pants. Now straight dudes also go for the street person/ holes look in jeans. Gay men also borrowed the new, longer shorts from the black community, and now even little boys are sporting gay-influenced shorts.

Khakis and Polos: Nicely dressed gay men have influenced straight America's tastes. You know the ones I mean, in the nice flat-front dress khakis and exquisitely expensive shirts. As one straight guy I know puts it: "What does the average gay guy look like? Sort of like a soccer dad, only maybe with a tighter shirt. It's hard to tell them apart." Richie Rich, one half of the gay design team Heatherette, agrees: "Right now a lot of gay men are dressing like straight men did last year, and a lot of straight men dress like gay men of a couple years back," he told *The Advocate* in April 2003. Seeing a straight man in a pink or purple shirt is no longer a rarity, even outside metrosexual circles. (A *metrosexual,* a term created by writer Mark Simpson, is a man who is straight but has gay habits and tastes.) Ah, the circle of fashion!

Body Hair: Consider the full, well-trimmed mustache of the late 1970s. It was born in the super-macho gay circles of New York and California, but it was made famous by Tom Selleck as Magnum. Take a look at old episodes of *Magnum, P.I.* Selleck, in his white short-shorts, tight T-shirts, and with big lip hair, appears "gay." But Magnum was the epitome of the straight, "sensitive-man" look in 1980, when the first episodes were shot.

In hip gay circles, mustaches were mostly out by the mid-eighties, replaced by goatees. Young gay men everywhere began sporting tiny, scraggly things in the crooks of their chins.

By the early 1990s, straight boys everywhere were having fun growing tiny bits of facial pubic hair—the minimalist goatee, also called a "soul patch," was de rigeur on the slacker coffee-house scene. The goatee came in with a vengeance and is still around in straight circles, along with the scruffy, unshaved look pioneered by gay male models and taken up with a vengeance by young, straight movie stars.

Hair dye is also in for straight guys—no one automatically thinks a guy is straight if he gets blond highlights. Perhaps it's the influence of Hollywood's new leading men, who now have their hair dyed all the time, both for roles and for fun. Brad Pitt was identified as "the ultimate metrosexual" by *Salon* e-zine. Before Stonewall, it would have been unthinkable to know that straight actors dyed their hair. Would Gary Cooper have gone blond for a role?

Gay men have also influenced the *absence* of hair on heterosexual men. The very definition of a metrosexual requires waxed eyebrows and body hair removal. No more hairy backs! The Fab Five on *Queer Eye for the Straight Guy* have let all of straight America watch as they wrangle the body hair of their clients. (Yes, there are many hairy gay guys—known as "bears" or "otters"—but it seems that the smooth-bodied gay men have captured the hairless look that straight men are now going for.)

Underwear: All straight women should fall down on their knees and thank homosexual men for creating and promoting sexy underwear for guys. Before 1990, most straight men didn't give a hoot about what they wore down there. Underwear was a drab item.

Then came the Mark Wahlberg underwear advertisements shot by gay photographer Bruce Weber. These Calvin Klein spreads were a milestone in male beefcake. Suddenly, "Marky Mark," a former boy-band singer and solo artist, was transformed into an erotic fantasy in his tighty-whiteys. I remember walking through Times Square sometime in the 1990s, when the famous half-naked Marky Mark billboard hung on Broadway. "I'm weak in the knees—it's so beautiful I can barely look," said my gay companion, Tom.

Weber went on to photograph many more attractive young men in their briefs and boxers, as did Richard Avedon. Designers such as Calvin Klein, Ralph Lauren, and Tommy Hilfiger promoted lines of sexy men's underwear. All of America became male underwear–obsessed. When then-presidential candidate Bill Clinton was interviewed on MTV in 1992, a female reporter asked him if he wore boxers or briefs. He weighed in with briefs. Is it just a coincidence that we first learned Clinton's underwear preference, and then, six years later, found out that his penis was crooked? It's as if he was doing a gradual presidential striptease.

Peacock Clothing: Wladziu Valentino Liberace switched from standard tuxedoes to white suits in his 1950s Las Vegas act so that his audiences could better see him on stage. In doing so, Liberace opened up the way for fancy duds for men. Of course, Liberace didn't stop at the plain white suit. He embellished it with rhinestones, velvet capes, feathers, and furs. Reportedly, Elvis admired the pianist and visited him often in his dressing room to talk about Vegas show business. What emerged was the "Fat Elvis" Vegas look of the late sixties and early seventies, a series of white pantsuits so effeminate that they made Elvis look curiously more masculine, like a guy who, even though squeezed into something that looked like his older sister's prom outfit, still oozed masculinity. Other hyper-masculine Vegas types such as Tom Jones and Engelbert Humperdinck were also affected by the Liberace style. The tradition of the straight entertainer dressed in sissy spangles continues to this day. Singer Chris Isaak is a great example.

Peacock clothes became popular for ordinary straight guys in the seventies—ruffled or blousy shirts, bright colors, shiny belts. The disco look and the leisure suits so many straight men wore toward the end of that decade had their origins in the gay disco look popularized by John Travolta in *Saturday Night Fever*.

The Amazing Nude Story of Abercrombie & Fitch

Every young straight man I know wears Abercrombie & Fitch. The clothing line is hugely popular with preteen and high-school boys. Many of them don't realize that Abercrombie clothing until very recently was a favorite choice of gay men.

Abercrombie started out with a straight-arrow clientele. Founded in 1892, the company was an outfitter of casual and sports clothing with a rather stuffy reputation. A kind of a cross between Eastern Mountain Sports and L.L.Bean, Abercrombie & Fitch supplied expeditions headed by Theodore Roosevelt and Richard Byrd.

But in 1997 Abercrombie & Fitch sexed up their quarterly catalog, filling the pages with seminude young men, and a few women tossed in for good measure. The catalog was so popular with the gay community that it spawned a pornographic parody website, Abercrombie & Filth.

Naturally, the new catalog attracted many gay customers who quickly made Abercrombie their new Gap. "A&F is the poster child for gay apparel," wrote Amanda Ryder in a 2000 InQueer Culture Review. A few years later, gay customers protested when the company reduced the number of male models in the catalog, saying that in deleting much of the homoerotic content, the company was turning its back on the homosexual market.

How gay was the content of the A&F Quarterly? Very. Issues featured themes such as 1999's "Surf Nekkid," with young nude men, photographed by Bruce Weber, holding surfboards in front of their genitals. A&F's Summer 2001 issue contained twelve pictures of topless girls and eleven pictures of completely nude boys, plus a two-page spread featuring nude men posed provocatively with their rear ends poking out of the shallow surf.

The company has consistently maintained that their audience for the sexy catalog is college students and older people. The state of Illinois tried to ban it, and many conservative commentators have mused that pictures of nude youths seemed a strange strategy for selling clothes. The catalog, like that of Victoria's Secret, is one of America's soft-porn standards.

When the *A&F Quarterly* was cancelled in December 2003, it made national news and inspired a lot of sighs from horny gay and straight Americans alike. Andrew, a gay blogger from Minneapolis, made it the lead in his daily journal.

> *The party is over for y'all who sit home on Saturday night jackin' it to Abercrombie & Fitch catalogues. They will be discontinuing it after pressure from fundamental prudes. I can't say I'm disappointed myself, but I do empathize with my gay compadres who will have to settle for XY magazine in order to fulfill those twink fantasies.*

I visited an Abercrombie store in a Los Angeles mall around the time the catalog was discontinued. Dewy semi-nude posters looking like *Queer Eye* versions of Hitler youth still graced its walls. The store was packed with straight young men and women buying up expensive fake-vintage T-shirts and jeans. Many of them were young, macho teenagers who probably use the word "gay" to mean lame. I wasn't going to be the one to tell them that their A&F wardrobe was shaped by a homosexual aesthetic.

Body Beautiful: Six-Pack Abs, Gay Gymrats, and Straight Boys

In Terrence McNally's 1991 play *Lips Together Teeth Apart*, two straight couples vacation on Fire Island in a house that had belonged to the brother of a main character, Sally, now deceased. The female guest, Chloe, spends most of her time

watching nearly naked gay men on the beach through binoc-
ulars. "You are so fucking hot, honey!" she says to a handsome boy she's been stalking. Then she turns to Sally and asks
why gay men are so much buffer than their straight counterparts. "[You] have to ask yourself: don't straight men have
eyes? Don't they occasionally look at themselves in the mirror? God knows, they expect us to."

Homosexual men have shown the way toward a new wave
of fitness worship. Working out at the gym, which previously
had been a strength issue for straight guys, has now become
more about aesthetics. The current emphasis on masculine ab-
domens and butts is a direct contribution of gay male culture,
which has indirectly benefited straight women. Women are
now being encouraged to objectify men's bodies in the same
way that men have "rated" female bodies over the years. The
gay culture's tendency to fetishize the male body has influenced straight female tastes. Everything now is all about pecs,
six-packs, and toned butts. (Note the bizarre scene in the Julia
Roberts movie *Runaway Bride*, where the ninety-year-old
grandmother says of Richard Gere's character, "I like his
tight buns!")

As usual, the fitness scene has witnessed the straight-
to-gay-to-straight cycle. When it comes to the sculpting of
straight male bodies, there has been a direct line from the
post–World War II bodybuilders such as Charles Atlas and
Jack LaLanne, to the homoerotic muscle magazines of the
1950s, to the gay men of today. And now straight men want to
look buff. Muscle magazines have always been considered
light gay porn, and yet have also been read by heterosexual

males. "In terms of impact as well as artistry," writes Thomas Waugh in his book about eroticism in male photography before Stonewall, "the current of physique eroticism that flourished in the postwar decades is one of the great achievements of gay culture."

The 1980s saw a surge in body awareness among gay men that eventually spilled over to the straight male scene. By the 1990s the stereotype of the gymrat emerged—the bemuscled young "twinks" who worked out constantly and frequented bars in gay ghettos such as Chelsea in New York or WeHo (West Hollywood) in Los Angeles. "If you're gay and live in New York and don't go to the gym, eventually they come for you," says Augusten Burroughs in his memoir, *Dry*. "The Gym Rats from Chelsea come in their Raymond Dragon tank tops and haul your ass into the back of a Yukon."

Body-conscious straight men—call them hetero gymrats, metrosexuals, or post-straights—are looking better all the time because they have begun emulating the gay emphasis on building a better physique. The bar has been raised, and the women in their lives, increasingly influenced by the gay body aesthetic, expect their men to be lean, muscular, and smooth-chested.

Men's Health magazine epitomizes the confluence of straight and gay body concerns. Started by health-conscious Rodale Press (publishers of *Prevention* magazine) as a fitness magazine for men, its circulation has expanded from only 90,000 in 1988 to more than 1.5 million today. Although the magazine dispenses heterosexual advice and has spawned its own sex guide for straight men, *Men's Health*, like *Gentle-*

man's Quarterly (*GQ*), has always had a homoerotic tone to its pages, especially in its featured fitness layouts and its cover shots. Chris Haines, in a 1998 *Salon* article, "The Sweaty-Chested Hunky-Boy Rag That Dare Not Speak Its Readers Name," dubbed *Men's Health* "the straight magazine gay men love to read." Of course, the magazine has a homoerotic feel to it—the covers, as Haines describes, feature "a new black-and-white photo of a handsome man with a perfectly chiseled (and inevitably shaved) torso in various stages of undress." But the more important point, I think, is that the magazine *is* read by both gay and straight men and that everyone feels fairly comfortable about it. Bodybuilding and fitness are now pansexual ideals.

From Greenwich Village to Target: Homo Style and Pop Culture

Can a Campbell's soup can be gay?

The tomato soup can certainly became gay by the time Andy Warhol transformed it in a series of paintings exhibited in Los Angeles in the summer of 1962. He took one of his mother's favorite processed lunch products and made it an American pop standard. Warhol's famous series of soup-can paintings and silk screenings are as iconic as the Mona Lisa, as are his garish portraits of American goddesses Marilyn Monroe, Jackie Kennedy Onassis, and Liz Taylor. Warhol was like a gay Norman Rockwell, taking the corny things Americans cherished and presenting them once again in a new guise.

Writing in the British Film Institute's magazine *Sight and Sound*, Mike O'Pray perfectly defined how Warhol's gay sensibility influenced American tastes:

> *The art critic Barbara Rose claims that Warhol was "the inventor of the lifestyle of the 60s." He did encapsulate all its idealism, experimentalism, arrogance (even, at times, its silliness) and most of what was understood as cool. Cool is precisely the hijacking of low and marginal culture into the mainstream—borrowing from the black ghettos, from the drug world of the streets, from gay clubs, from S&M dress. Warhol was an artist operating in a tiny elite avant-garde in New York, but only Picasso in the modern period has had such universal recognition.*

In studying pop culture over the last forty years, all roads lead to the bewigged Warhol, a mysterious figure who loved camp and swish and celebrity of any persuasion. His influence took many forms—films, art, fashion, and commercial products. He worshipped the rich and famous, and yet he also made the idea of celebrity accessible to everyone. His prophetic line, "In the future, everyone will be famous for fifteen minutes," has become nearly true; it was uttered almost forty years before the glut of reality television shows such as *Survivor, The Bachelor,* and *American Idol.*

We do owe much of how we see our culture to Warhol, and yet his major contribution, more than his art, was his penchant for commercialization. He exploited many merchandising opportunities during his lifetime, and encouraged the younger artist Keith Haring to do the same. Haring's strange graffiti-inspired drawings of men, angels, babies, hearts, and dogs have become ubiquitous through greeting cards, tote bags, shower curtains, and even sheets. In 1986, four years before his death, Haring opened Pop Shop in Manhattan's SoHo, selling household items and stationery featuring his art. The art world was in an uproar about how this young, edgy artist had sold out. Yet Haring's move paved the way for many other artists and designers, helping to blur the line between the serious art world and pop-culture consumerism.

In 2001 both he and Andy Warhol were named in a list of the "richest deceased celebrities" in *Forbes* magazine. Haring's estate earned $4 million in 2001 alone. (Haring died of AIDS in 1990.) In the same year, Andy Warhol's estate made more than $8 million licensing his art. (Warhol died in 1987 during a gallbladder operation.)

Gay men and the gay sensibility created pop culture, and now homosexual designers continue to make their mark on what Americans want to buy. Thousands of straight high-school- and college-age kids furnish their bedrooms and dorm rooms with gay designer Todd Oldham's hip striped bedroom collection for the mass-market chain Target. Oldham, who once designed couture shirts and hip hotels, took his inspiration from the disco seventies when he first began designing for Target in 2003.

"True to form, Oldham has created products with pattern and personality to spare," wrote Marge Colborn, the *Detroit News* design editor. "He's reinterpreted camouflage, played with multicolor stripes, put a fancy spin on stars and brought vintage varsity letters into the 21st century."

On a blunter note, Matt, a gay blogger who works for the New School University in New York City, posted this note when the collection debuted: "Leave it to Oldham to take a classic gay fantasy, the dorm room, and make it perfectly palpable [sic] for mass American tastes. I couldn't believe my eyes when I saw all the crap Target was peddling under the Todd Oldham label. Most of it is simply repurposed plastic hangers and plates in neon colors. But now that I've seen it in over half the rooms of my dorm, I have to admit it's pretty stylish."

Target has also recruited the wonderfully swishy Isaac Mizrahi to bring style to its women's-wear collection. Mizrahi, a former couture designer, was the star of a witty, funny documentary, *Unzipped*, filmed by his then-boyfriend, Douglas Keeve. The film follows him throughout his nutty quest to base his 1994 collection of dresses and coats on the silent movie *Nanook of the North*. Now *that's* gay.

After his design firm failed, Mizrahi started moving closer to the mass market, landing his own talk show on the Oxygen network. But he made the final leap into America's homes and closets by signing up with Target. In 2003 he announced the debut of the Isaac Mizrahi for Target line of women's clothing and accessories. "My clothes have always celebrated the style of American women of all ages and all walks of life," said Mizahi in his announcement. "Now, through my partnership with Target, I can offer my designs to more women than ever before at accessible prices."

In 2004, Target began airing a campy commercial with Mizrahi as a lounge singer, crooning the old Frank Sinatra standard "I Believe in You" to the many women clustered around his piano. Could there be a more perfect metaphor for how gay designers have become safe for straight America?

Chapter 6

Butts and Cocks:
Gay Men
and the
Future of Sex

I just don't want to be known as the "up-the-butt" girl.
—Kristin Davis, playing Charlotte on *Sex and the City*

It pisses straight people off when I mention this, but the simple fact that I'm gay—the blessing of my homosexuality—was all the preparation I needed to give sex advice. Gay people know more about sex than straight people do, have more sex than straight people do, and are better at it than straight people are.

—Dan Savage, sex columnist, in "Savage Love"

Men are men. Men generally do not want to wait to have sex. It's not like with women. It's a lot easier for gay men to have sex. Gay men are very fortunate in that respect.

—Steven, from *Real World Las Vegas*,
talking to *The Advocate* magazine

The real issue is not that heterosexuals will be tempted to engage in homosexual sexual activity . . . but that they will be drawn to more flexible norms that gay people, excluded from social structures created by heterosexuality, have created for their own lives. These include less restrictive gender roles; non-monogamous intimate relationships and more freedom for sexual experimentation; family units that are chosen, not biological; and new models for parenting. But most importantly, homosexuality offers a vision of sexual pleasure completely divorced from the burden of reproduction: sex for its own sake, a distillation of the pleasure principle.

—Michael Bronski in *Culture Clash:
The Making of Gay Sensibility*

Do gay men have better sex than straight folks? And if so, are they teaching heterosexuals how to get up to speed?

The so-called sexual revolution of the late 1960s was really just a set of personal skirmishes that initially succeeded in freeing heterosexuals to enjoy sex outside of marriage. In its first phase, the revolution also granted women the right to have orgasms and to enjoy intercourse, which from the vantage point of the twenty-first century seems like a ridiculously simplistic notion.

But thankfully, just as straight people began to lose their zeal for fighting to be sexually free and became complacent about the gains they had made, homosexuals took up the cause. In the eighties, particularly as gay men started to come out in greater numbers, even the sad onset of the AIDS epidemic could not dampen the refreshing contributions homosexuals made to American sexuality. Much of the diversity and innovation in straight sex lives today is due to these gay influences. Straight America is more comfortable with oral and anal sex, pornography, bondage, sex toys, and bisexuality than it has ever been before.

Straight and Gay: Madonna's Big Book of Sex

The literary and visual apotheosis of the gay/straight sex connection was Madonna's slightly twisted coffee-table book *Sex,* published in 1992. Although Madonna now prefers being known as a children's author, I keep imagining little Lourdes and Rocco's surprise the first time someone shows them mommy's other book, the one she wrote before she discovered motherhood and the kabbalah.

I recall being at many straight parties where the book *Sex* was passed around; it was the homoerotic photographs that both terrified and titillated at the same time. There was Madonna with two boys servicing her. In another photo, a man dominates another man wearing a black latex hood. And the party guests definitely enjoyed checking out the montage of naked boys having sex. The most provocative shot, I think, is the one in which Madonna is on her knees, kissing a man's ass. Well, kissing is sort of a euphemism. She's actually licking his asshole. She's "rimming" him, although most straight people in 1992 did not know that term. Now the term is becoming common, and the gay attitude toward anal play is becoming more of a presence in heterosexual bedrooms.

In her omni-sexual poise in the late eighties and early nineties, Madonna was a pioneer. She was the first homosexual icon to interact with her audience sexually (well, unless you count Judy Garland's marriages to gay men). She borrowed from the gay male culture and informed her fans of worlds they didn't know before. She was dressed by Jean Paul Gaultier, the bitchiest designer of all time. Who else but a gay man could invent such aggressive lingerie? The leather conical bras threatened to impale anyone nearby; the chains and fishnets were straight from a bad Weimar Republic porno flick.

Madonna during her depraved years was a bit like Marco Polo bringing back noodles from China to Italy, and we have a lot to thank her for. She heterosexualized gay sex, and we are all the richer for it.

Girls and Gays, and the Sex Tips They Share

When the television show *Sex and the City* first aired, many critics mentioned that it featured women talking in a realistic way about sex to their female friends. I don't believe it. The four main characters—Charlotte, Miranda, Samantha, and Carrie—talk to one another *the way I talk to my gay male friends*. I would never discuss anal sex, sex toys, penis size, or other intimate topics with my girlfriends, but all of these topics emerge frequently in conversations with my gay boyfriends. My gay pals talk about hard-ons and discuss kissing in much more depth than my female friends. They're also nonchalant about sex toys in a way that the average female population is not.

Sex and the City was created by Darren Starr, a gay producer, and was overseen by another gay writer, Michael Patrick King. Gay males as well as straight women often scripted it. Some commentators have gone so far as to suggest that the four main female characters are really gay men disguised as women.

I disagree, but I do think that the female characters are inflected with a certain gay male spirit. They've been given the freedom to talk about sex constantly, which is not something women do very well.

The show has become a catalyst for deeper sexual communication among women. Now that *Sex and the City* has run its course through six seasons of popularity, I've seen how it can start intimate sexual conversations among women. Friends who would never be as open before about all sorts of sexual issues will discuss them if they know a *Sex and the City* character has talked about them.

The comedy series devoted an entire episode to anal sex; another episode featured a discussion about anal/oral sex. "Are we talking assalingus here?" asked Miranda at one point. One episode had Samantha despairing over her lover's tiny penis. On another show, Samantha confided, "I'm dating a guy with the funkiest tasting spunk."

Straight people are getting fresh ideas and advice about sex from the gay world in many media. The country's most popular syndicated sex-advice column is "Savage Love," penned by an openly gay man, Dan Savage. Savage, who has written several books, is now the editor of Seattle's alternative newspaper *The Stranger.* Most of the questions he answers are from heterosexuals. Savage answers them in a delightfully bitchy, assertive way. For example, a father writes in and asks what he should do now that he has walked in on his son, who was masturbating in the bathroom. Says Savage: "Your son is 14 fucking years old, you moron, of course he's beating off in his room. Where did you beat off when you were 14? Buckingham Palace?"

In an earlier incarnation of his column, Savage had his readers address him "Hey, Faggot," emphasizing his self-deprecating gay wit. He frequently offers in-depth advice on specific acts and techniques that I don't think a straight columnist would attempt, such as dildo or anal penetration, fisting, and specific techniques for cunnilingus.

A Hard Pill for Swallowing, or How Gays Invented Recreational Viagra

Like everyone else in the country, I heard about Viagra from magazine and newspaper articles when it was first put on the market in 1998. The "little blue pill" that promised instant erections seemed sort of sad, or embarrassing, when it was first introduced. Boyfriends and husbands of my straight friends feigned disinterest in the breakthrough—surely they didn't need a drug to get it up. Yet only six months after Pfizer had introduced it, I began hearing about the pleasure potential of Viagra from my *gay* male friends. "Oh my god, oh my godddd!" said one of my friends. "It's like you're nineteen again! I had several new admirers at the bar the other night."

I tip my hat (or something else, fill in the blank here, since this *is* a sex chapter) to gay guys for their pharmaceutical ingenuity. They co-opted a serious medicine with negative associations of aging and waning virility, and made it into a party drug. Whereas many heterosexual men saw Viagra and thought, *A drug to help me get it up—am I that feeble?*, gay men saw it and said, "Hey! A drug that will help me stay hard all night! I want it!"

By 2001, a San Francisco study was warning of the dangers of recreational Viagra in the gay community. Viagra had left the regular medical world to become a "club drug" that could banish the erectile dysfunction associated with crystal meth, cocaine, ecstasy, Special K, alcohol, and other regularly abused party drugs. The study, conducted by the San Francisco Department of Health, showed that gay and bisexual men were four times more likely to use Viagra recreationally than were heterosexual men.

As in so many other social cycles, straight men in their teens and twenties began catching on to Viagra a few years after their homosexual counterparts. "Gay men are simply ahead on the social learning curve," reported Bob Condor in the *Chicago Tribune* in 2003. He interviewed Dr. Abraham Morgentaler, a Harvard Medical School physician who studies sexual dysfunction. "One thing that is remarkable is it has all happened without anybody paying much attention," said Morgentaler, who also runs a clinic where college-age men try to "score" Viagra.

He notes that there is a lively underground Viagra scene among young men, who buy or trade "six-packs" of Viagra samples that have been distributed free to doctors. Even though Pfizer, which markets the drug, insists that it is for erectile dysfunction and not for recreational use, the party six-pack conjures up other "great American male images," says Morgentaler. "The first, of course, is the six-pack of beer. The second refers to the highly desired set of abdominal muscles."

So, after being reinvented by the male gay social scene, Viagra has become firmly ensconced as a club drug at heterosexual raves and at straight dance venues. Viagra and its generic counterpart are easily available on the Internet without a prescription, and although that wide availability could change in the future, Viagra and newer erectile-dysfunction drugs such as Levitra are becoming assimilated into the sex lives of healthy, functional gay and straight men entranced by the special effects the medicines produce. With other such drugs on the horizon, we can also count on gay male pioneers to experiment with them recreationally, however risky that could be.

The Cult of the Penis and the Deification of the Blow Job

Hey, Faggot:
What is the difference between cocksucking, blow jobs, and fellatio?

—Unsigned

Hey, Unsigned,

"Cocksucking" is what my boyfriend's good at; "blow
jobs" are what my sister gives; and "fellatio" is what my
mom does.

—from Dan Savage's sex column, "Savage Love"

"Swallowing!" says one gay man I know, talking of fellatio.
"It's not like we invented the issue of whether to swallow or
not to swallow," says my friend, "but we definitely brought it
more to the attention of the straight world."

I like to think of the nineties as the Blow-Job Decade, a
time when straight and gay trends came together to result in
an American obsession with the phallus.

At the very least, it was the period of time when the penis,
heterosexual and homosexual, came out of the closet. In 1994
we were all shocked to find John Wayne Bobbit's pecker at the
side of the road; it was only then that the word "penis" began
to appear frequently in mainstream newspapers and magazines. Meanwhile, anecdotal reports of middle-schoolers in-
dulging in fellatio became commonplace and appeared in
reputable sources such as *The New York Times* and *The Washington Post*. The cult of the penis was on the rise.

By 1998, we were all able to read detailed descriptions of
President Clinton's distinctively shaped phallus. It's significant that our president committed adultery not via ho-hum
missionary-position sex, but with abbreviated incidents of
fellatio. In fact, the Clinton/Monica Lewinsky scandal rede-
fined sex for Americans. Although the president put his penis
in a young woman's mouth and a cigar into one of her orifices,

he at first denied that he'd had sex with her. But by gay standards (and also by many straight standards), what Bill Clinton and Monica Lewinsky did together was definitely "sex."

I've talked to liberal gay men who see Bill's penchant for oral sex as reassuringly deviant. One man went so far as to say, "I feel that he is an honorary gay man, in a way."

The glorification of the penis has long been a gay male thing. Or, at least, "nice girls" weren't supposed to talk about how a penis looks, tastes, or feels. But thanks to a healthy cross-pollination between gay and straight cultures, women are now freer to objectify the organ, too.

In 1997, I was invited to an Easter-egg-dying party hosted by a gay friend. One of the guests had an advance copy of a film her brother had directed for HBO's *Real Sex* show, which featured male strippers with penises more than twelve inches long. It was a strange but very merry party as we decorated our eggs and watched the guys whip out their giant cocks.

Layer upon layer of sexual audience and attitudes was involved.

First, our viewing audience at the party was made up of single men and women, both gay and straight, and of gay and heterosexual couples. Of course, no children were in attendance.

Within the short film we were watching, the audience was African-American women, who frequented the featured strip club in North Philadelphia. The well-endowed performers, said the woman who had brought the tape to our party, were widely known to be mostly gay men, although they were performing for straight women.

There we sat, clutching our female egg fertility symbols but glued to the screen as we watched the yang to our yin— giant penises dancing away in close-up. It was a strange confluence of gay and straight culture. For me it was a watershed moment in the millennial cult of the penis.

There's an old, really bad joke that was told to me by my misogynist Uncle Bernie. A woman goes to the eye doctor, complaining that her vision is bad. The doctor holds up one finger, then two, and then his whole hand. The woman claims she can't see the fingers or the hand. Then the doctor unzips his pants, and the woman says she can see his penis. Says the doctor, "Lady, that's your problem: You're cockeyed!"

The straight women and men of America have all gone cockeyed, if we can believe the anecdotal evidence. Being good in bed now requires a lot of oral sex expertise. In towns and cities all across America, heterosexual women have been making great strides in their ability to talk about blow jobs, and in their dedication to improving their fellatio skills. There are courses around the country in the art of the blow job, taught by gay men as well as by straight women. There are Tupperware-style parties in which neighborhood women sell dildos and vibrators.

Here's a course description for Fellatio 101 listed by Joy Toyz, a woman-owned sex-toy shop in Montreal:

This course is a journey to explore the various male erogenous zones, focussing on the oral stimulation of the genitals. Study tried & true favourites, including "Classic Fellatio," plus a host of assorted intermediate & advanced techniques. Discussions and exercises allow an awakening to a more diverse and playful stimulation of a man's body. This course is offered in both English & French. A male sex artist caters his talents for this women's-only class.

In 2003, a *Queer as Folk* episode on Showtime highlighted the gay man/straight woman fellatio connection. Sharon Gless, playing the middle-age mother/waitress Debbie, was unexpectedly asked out on a date. Realizing that she hadn't had sex in quite a while, she enlists advice from her son's gay friends. Ted and Emmett show up with a bagful of dildos and proceed to teach her everything they know about the perfect blow job.

When her new boyfriend, a conservative middle-age cop, comments that she must have had a lot of practice performing oral sex, she gets insulted and throws him out of the house. Her tutors, Ted and Emmett, eventually have to go down to the police station to explain, not very modestly, that they, gay men, were responsible for her fellatio talents.

As both gay and straight reviewers have pointed out, *Queer as Folk* bears little resemblance to reality. Pittsburgh doesn't really have the glamorous gay scene depicted on the show, and the club where the boys hang out, Babylon, seems to be part Land of Oz and part some demented teenager's vision of an eighties disco joint. Since the popular series focuses on a very narrow segment of the population—young, urban gay men who spend a lot of time dancing and taking drugs—it's taken a lot of flack from gay activists. Yet straight women have connected to this show in great numbers. Why? As far as Showtime executives can tell, straight women like the gay sex scenes. "It was intended as a gay show written for a gay audience," explained Daniel Lipman to the press when they released the viewing figures. Lipman, along with Ron Cowan, created the American version of the British TV hit. "It has amazed everyone that there's such a crossover."

The show's 2003 finale attracted an audience that was 50 percent straight female. Mindy Newby, a California insurance underwriter, told *Newsweek* that she initially found the homosexual sex scenes "shocking," but "then it became incredibly sexy. Straight men should watch it."

The show has become a craze among many straight women, who organize all-female *Queer as Folk* dinner parties. An informal poll of my straight girlfriends who watch the show confirms this. "It's just so hot," says my friend Sarah, a computer consultant in Wilmington, Delaware. I agree. I think we are beginning to see a trend in which heterosexual women will become turned on by male homosexuality as much as traditional straight men have been excited by lesbian sex. All of the sex on *Queer as Folk* is either anal or oral—what does this say about the average female viewer's sexual preoccupations?

The success of the book *Sex Tips for Straight Women from a Gay Man* further proves that heterosexual women respect and solicit the gay male perspective on sex. The advice book, by Dan Anderson and Maggie Berman, has been in print for more than five years, and is available not only at traditional bookstores, but at hip chain shops such as Urban Outfitters. It's very penis-oriented, with a whole chapter on size, shape, and the presence or absence of foreskin. One chapter explores the world of the hand job, and another is devoted completely to fellatio, with sections on "BJ Basics," "Hummers," "Tinglers," and even "Dick Whipping" (lightly smacking the penis against one's face).

Oral sex has not always been part of most Americans' sexual repertoire. According to a 1994 study of American sexual practices, only a minority of women over age fifty had ever performed oral sex. Among women younger than thirty-five, however, more than three quarters had done so. Most men, whatever their age, had been both givers and receivers of oral sex.

Straight people have become oral. How much of their newfound fixation do they owe to their gay counterparts?

Straight People Become Less Anal-Retentive

"Attention all straight men! This is a call to arms," wrote ex-porn actress Tristan Taomarino in *The Village Voice* at the turn of the last century. "There is something you need to learn how to do," she continued, "something that can transform your life . . . You've got something to pick up from your gay brothers. And it's not just those fashion and decorating tips you marvel about on *Will & Grace*. . . . There is a craze sweeping the nation, and you oughta know about it. It's ass fucking—with you on the receiving end."

Whoa.

Anal sex has become the newest craze among heterosexuals, with both men and women vying to be on the receiving end. It's not as if gay men invented anal sex, or that no heterosexuals tried it before the 1990s—after all, statistics show that more heterosexuals than homosexuals have practiced anal sex. And it's a fallacy to think that all gay men engage in anal sex—many never do. Still, though, it's as if the heterosexual practice has been "outed" and made easier to talk about in a gay-friendly environment. This is interesting, since butt-fucking has traditionally been the greatest fear of homophobic people.

The taboo aspect of anal sex between a man and a woman has made it a popular heterosexual porn subject for years. But recently the idea of a man penetrating a woman's anus is becoming more "normal" or mainstream. Two heterosexual male pornographers, Buttman (John Staggliano) and Seymore Butts (Adam Glasser), have done the most to focus on the female rear end in their pornographic video businesses. Between them they've sold hundreds of thousands of titles such as *Where the Sun Don't Shine*, *Tushy Tahitian Style*, *Wise Crack*, and *International Tushy*. Adam Glasser has even been the focus of a reality series on Showtime, *Family Business*, in which he's depicted as a small-time businessman who just happens to shoot films about anal sex and female ejaculation.

Now the anal "craze," if you want to call it that, is going

into a new phase. The final anal frontier is being broached by heterosexual men. More and more straight men are discovering the joys of prostate stimulation, and are asking for help in learning how to get stimulated.

The *Bend Over, Boyfriend* videotape series has sold thousands of copies via the Internet and heterosexual sex-toy catalogs. Conceived, written, and produced by women, the tapes feature Dr. Carol Queen and her boyfriend showing heterosexual America how a gal can penetrate her man with a strap-on dildo.

Anal sex toys are now popular in straight markets, too. A gay male friend was the first person to tell me about the Aneros. "You should check this out," he said, "because it's being sold mostly to straight guys."

The Aneros is a plastic shoehorn-like insert that fits snugly into the anus and presses on the prostate, enhancing the male orgasm. Grant Stoddard, the heterosexual "science" columnist for the erotic online magazine *Nerve*, was assigned to experiment with the Aneros, and despite being terrified beforehand, gave the device a glowing review after getting off to a rocky start:

> But after a while, I lost patience with the instruction manual—which read like an unabridged copy of the Talmud—and I decided to go with my instincts and what I'd gleaned from the website. The idea is that with some practice, you can reach orgasm just by squeezing your sphincter, without even touching your penis.
>
> After about ten minutes of serious squeezing, I was to-

tally tuckered out and starting to feel a bit silly, what with the toy's handle protruding like an albino ram's horn from between my cheeks. I admitted defeat and rolled onto my back to bang one out in the old-school fashion. Lying on my back must have shifted the position of the toy, because I almost dropped sauce immediately and had to concentrate hard not to. When I came shortly thereafter, the feeling was much more intense than normal.

The Aneros website is chock-full of delighted testimonials from heterosexual men. Most of them repeatedly emphasize how cool their wives think the Aneros is, and how virile they are within their romantic, heterosexual relationships.

Congratulations, heterosexuals! You've been touched by an anal. And you should thank gay men for bringing up the subject.

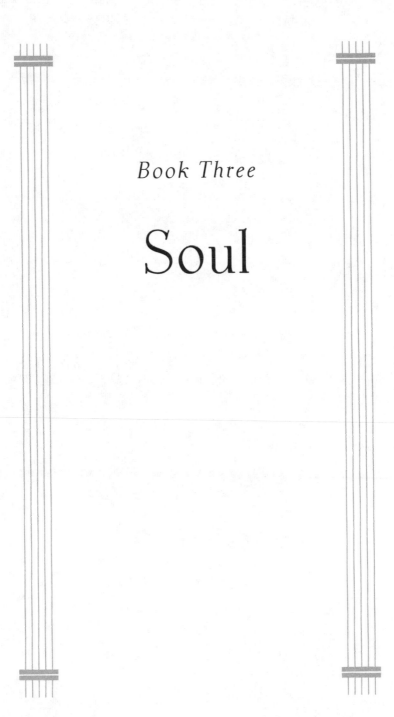

Book Three

Soul

Chapter 7

Movies:
My Favorite
Things

Because I just went gay all of a sudden!
—Cary Grant as paleontologist David Huxley
in *Bringing Up Baby*, explaining why he is
wearing a pink-feathered negligee

Thanks to the silver screen, your neurosis has got style.
—Donald in *The Boys in the Band* by Mart Crowley

Queers are just better! I'd be so proud if you was a fag and had a nice beautician boyfriend. . . . I worry that you'll work in an office, have children, celebrate wedding anniversaries. The world of a heterosexual is a sick and boring life.

—Aunt Ida (Edith Massey)
in John Waters's *Female Trouble*

Come out, come out, wherever you are . . .
—Glinda the Good Witch in *The Wizard of Oz*

Gay men have always been enthusiastic cineastes, with a dedication to the silver screen that knows no bounds. Perhaps there is no place better than the movies to pause awhile and examine what makes something "gay," even if it was created by straight people. An episode of *Six Feet Under* showed a group of gay men sitting around, making outrageous comments while watching *The Bad Seed*, the 1956 movie about a precocious girl murderer. The film, made in all earnest, screams "camp."

The *Bad Seed* was on television often when I was a little girl, and it both terrified and titillated me. Here was a very rotten little girl, Rhoda, played by the blonde darling Patty McCormack, who seemed to have no remorse for the murders she had committed. I took *The Bad Seed* seriously as a child of ten, but I can see now why it's a camp classic: Little Rhoda's constant and ominous piano renditions of "Clair de Lune," the janitor's ominous yet hilarious threat that Rhoda will be electrocuted in a special little pink electric chair for girls, and

Eileen Heckart's over-the-top performance as the drunken bereaved mother of one of Rhoda's victims (a little boy who had won a school medal Rhoda coveted) all merge to create a kitschy masterpiece of gay cinema.

While staying up late watching television on summer evenings, I was gradually inoculated with a gay film sensibility without even knowing it. A lot of the movies had strong, evil women who appealed to me (and, I now understand, to little gay boys, too). I loved *I Want to Live!*, the 1958 movie featuring Susan Hayward as a slutty party gal, Barbara Graham, unjustly accused of murder. She's tough from the beginning, in an early interrogation scene:

> *Police lieutenant: You know she's been murdered, don't you?*
> *Barbara Graham: Yeah. So was Julius Caesar. I didn't know him, either.*

Late-night mid-sixties television was a treasure trove of movies made in the 1930s, 1940s, and 1950s. And even after school, kids would be fed films from long ago. In the New York area, where I lived until I was eight years old, Channel 9 ran a daily Million Dollar Movie. Every afternoon, the theme song from *Gone with the Wind* would come on, and then the show. But here's the kicker: It would be the same picture every day for a whole week. That's how I got to memorize lines from the 1933 *King Kong* and identify with Fay Wray. Years later, in college, at the late-night shows, I immediately understood Dr. Frank-N-Furter's musings during a number in *The Rocky Horror Picture Show*: "Whatever happened to Fay Wray?" And when I read queer interpretations of the "encoded" gay content of that movie, and of the allegory of the monster who was sensitive enough to fall in love, and yet was exploited for being grotesque and different, I could see the point exactly.

All movies are gay, but some are gayer than others. Not surprisingly, the gay movie canon has had an enormous impact on straight culture.

What Makes a Film Queer?

The homosexual sensibility in film is fairly rampant, and it's a large part of what makes movies both intimate and surreal at the same time.

Trying to put one's finger on the gayness that emanates from certain movies could make a person go crazy. There are two aspects to the gay vibes some films give off.

1. Encoding, or subtext.

Working on the assumption that queerness is in the eye of the beholder, almost any film can be subject to a queer interpretation. "*Top Gun* is the gayest movie ever made," said one anonymous commentator on a gay website. He cited the homoerotic flyboy situation, the camaraderie of the men, the prettiness of the guys, and, in particular, one shower scene. "If you look at the subtext of *X-Men* and *X2*," E! Online columnist Anderson Jones told the *New York Daily News*, "they're two of the gayest movies ever made. They're [constructed] with an awareness of what people on the outside go through. They take their differences and blow them up into superpowers, and that's one of the main reasons they work."

2. Homosexual writers, actors, directors, and producers.

Gay movie people either create or are attracted to a certain type of material, or certain styles. Gay writer Hanif Kureishi's *My Beautiful Laundrette* would seem gay even if it didn't feature a gay romance. The movie version of *Grease* gets its gay vibe, I think, from the late flamboyant producer Alan Carr.

Director Todd Haynes (*Velvet Goldmine, Far from Heaven*) was asked by the *Seattle Intelligencer* if it was fair to say that the fifties melodramas of Douglas Sirk and others had a gay sensibility. "Yes, homosexuality, while behind-the-scenes, was indeed evident in the making of the films—as it was, arguably, in the aesthetics of many directors of 'women's films,' like George Cukor and Vincente Minnelli," said Haynes. "While thematically restricted, a gay or 'feminine' aesthetic was free to pervade the profuse visual style: the clothes, the colors, the lavish decor."

Has anyone ever noticed how Todd Haynes speaks in full paragraphs? As difficult as it is to define a gay aesthetic, he comes closest of all the gay directors working today.

"Women's films" is only one category in which to explore a film's gayness, but let's start with that and add a few more.

When Films Scream Gay, Gay, Gay: A Genre Guide

Strong women, crybaby situations:
Women's films were not too far away from what are now dismissed (or cherished) as chick flicks. Early and more recent movies with strong female characters and tear-jerking sensibilities include *Mildred Pierce, Stella Dallas, Mrs. Miniver, Little Women, The Best Years of Our Lives, All About Eve, Sunset Boulevard, Picnic, Splendor in the Grass,* and *Magnificent Obsession*. Newer versions include *Steel Magnolias, Terms of Endearment, Thelma & Louise, Stepmom,* and *One True Thing*.

Anything starring Judy Garland:
Yes, younger gay men would rather die than be a Judy Queen, but it's true that Garland's movies project some sort of gay essence. The Queer Masterpiece *The Wizard of Oz* is among them, as well as *A Star Is Born, Meet Me in St. Louis,* and all those "Hey, kids, let's put on a show!" pictures with Mickey Rooney.

Anything featuring Joan Crawford or Bette Davis:
These gals are the undisputed queens of gay cinema, and their legacy continues because of two rather late developments: First, their appearance together in *What Ever Happened to Baby Jane?* in 1964 was a high-camp romp that solidified their larger-than-life images for future generations. Second,

Faye Dunaway's performance as Joan Crawford in *Mommie Dearest* was more Crawford than Crawford, and succeeded in making "No more wire hangers!" a gay battle cry for domestic civilization. *Mommie Dearest* was in 1981—thank goodness the wire hanger phrase came along and replaced another line that was parodied all the time from *The Goodbye Girl* (1977), Richard Dreyfuss's hammy heterosexual line, "And I don't—like—the panties—hanging—on—the rod."

Anything starring Madonna:

She was the "It" girl of the 1980s, starting with *Desperately Seeking Susan*, progressing through the dismal *Who's That Girl?*, and then moving on to *Evita*. Madonna's ultimate faghag movie, *The Next Best Thing*, where she got to nail the only gay leading man in show business, Rupert Everett, was a really stinky picture. She was so bad that she almost made Rupert look like a heterosexual. But I guess it was just to even things out: Madonna made Warren Beatty's *Dick Tracy* gay just by singing that fabulous song "Sooner or Later" by Stephen Sondheim. And Madonna's documentary, *Truth or Dare*, was postmodern gay at its finest.

All movie musicals:

At eleven I attended a slumber party where we watched the MGM musical *Seven Wives for Seven Brothers*. All those boys in tight trousers turned me on. But now, when I look back at that film, it seems homoerotic. Likewise, *Kismet, South Pacific, Singin' in the Rain, An American in Paris, Gigi, My Fair Lady*, and all the Fred Astaire movies. *White Christmas*, starring Bing Crosby and Sir Laurence Olivier's boyfriend, Danny Kaye, features that wonderful drag number, "Sisters." Venturing into more contemporary territory, the movie of the musical *Cabaret*, starring Michael York and Liza Minnelli, is *very* gay, as is the new *Chicago*, which was directed by openly gay Rob Marshall.

Camp and kitsch:

The promotional tagline for *Valley of the Dolls* (1967): "In the Valley of the Dolls, it's instant turn-on . . . dolls to put you to sleep at night, kick you awake in the morning, make life seem great—instant love, instant excitement, ultimate hell!" Geez— can you get any campier? Other camp extravaganzas include sword-and-sandal flicks, B-movies, Sinbad the Sailor movies, and biblical epics of any kind. The original *Planet of the Apes* movies were really gay, so gay that the gay characters in the comedy *All Over the Guy* (2001) felt the need to discuss it:

> *Eli: Well, you've got a half-naked Charlton Heston in a cage—*
> *Tom: Where he belongs.*
> *Eli: Plus my huge crush on Roddy McDowell, and those cute little leather outfits . . . that, my friend, is a gay pre-teen Happy Meal.*

Any movie derived from a Tennessee Williams play or short story:

"*Suddenly Last Summer* is cinema's gay horn of plenty, a fabulous gothic thriller and a pantheon of renowned gay artists and classic gay icons," says Mark Adnum on his website OutRate.net, where he reviews DVDs. Even if you recall only part of the plot—Katharine Hepburn is trying to persuade Montgomery Clift to perform a lobotomy on her distraught daughter, Elizabeth Taylor, who is obviously about to spill the beans about her brother's perverted sexuality—you know that we're in high-strung homosexual territory. The script, by Tennessee Williams and Gore Vidal, delivers enough camp and dysfunctionality to satisfy any gay or straight audience. And there's plenty more where that came from—just check out Anna Magnani and Burt Lancaster as campy would-be lovers with a fixation on skin drawings in *The Rose Tattoo*.

Anything written and directed by John Waters:

Starting out at the fringe of nowhere (i.e., Baltimore), John Waters eventually traveled into the brains of Middle America. His films with the drag queen Divine—*Pink Flamingos, Female Trouble, Polyester, Hairspray*—celebrated the oddness of transvestite white-trash culture. His dyspeptic view of high-school culture has finally penetrated the straight world via the Broadway production of *Hairspray*.

High-concept romantic movies:

Consider the all-time seventies doomed romance: Barbra Streisand and Robert Redford in *The Way We Were*. It meant so much to me in 1973, when I was just barely out of high school. I identified with Streisand's career aspirations—to be a writer—and also with her matter-of-fact approach to sex.

(In one scene she inserts her diaphragm and then climbs on top of Redford, who falls asleep while they are having sex.) And, of course, there's that killer, schmaltzy song, warbled by Barbra herself. I hope I haven't put it into your head just by mentioning it. The movie is popular among baby boomer gay guys simply because of Barbra's presence. Yet I'd never checked out who wrote it. It was by the gay writer Arthur Laurents, who wrote the books for *Gypsy* and *West Side Story*. Finding that out was an "aha!" moment for me. In the movie, Streisand and Redford break up because of Hollywood black-listing—Redford can't go along with Streisand's extreme politics. The plot has a gay sense of alienation and a gay version of a strong woman who can't be tamed. But once again, as with so many movies, plays, and books, I'm amazed at how Laurents, a gay man, created a template for how women should feel about doomed heterosexual romance.

And what about the gay Italian director Franco Zeffirelli? He created one of the most romantic movies of all time, the very lush *Romeo and Juliet,* the first modern version of the Shakespeare story in which the sexual focus of the camera was the male lover, Romeo, rather than the lovely Juliet. Jan Stuart, writing in *The Advocate,* said that Zeffirelli "gave *Romeo and Juliet* the 64-Crayola sparkle of an MGM musical." But I think that what he really provided was an intense homoerotic view in the love scenes—the camera's gaze rested squarely on Leonard Whiting as Romeo, with his beautiful body and face often flooding the screen. In 1968, we girls all swooned over Zeffirelli's Romeo—it makes perfect sense that he was created by a gay auteur.

Retrofitted projects:

The gayest movie I've seen in the last few years is *Down with Love*, an homage to the Doris Day/Rock Hudson comedies, with Renée Zellwegger as Doris, Ewan McGregor as Rock, and Frasier's David Hyde Pierce in the ambisexual Tony Randall role. In this category of gay recycled movie material, I also nominate the witty film rehabs performed by writer Paul Rudnick, who made the new *Addams Family* movies into total camp experiences.

Horror films:

Gay directors virtually invented the horror genre. Starting with E. W. Murnau, the director of the early silent Dracula flicks in the 1920s, and continuing with James Whale, the gay director of the original Frankenstein movies, the horror film has always had a definite homosexual inflection. Says film critic Richard Barrios in his book about gay movies and actors, *Screened Out*:

> *The gayness of Whale's horror films is seldom on the surface, for his dry theatrical wit rarely permitted anything so overt. Instead, there are hints and symbols, coded references. . . . Whales' misfit outsiders pitted against hostile mobs, his unholy same-sex friendships, and his amused skewing of hetero norms all form a base camp for queer film theory.*

It's interesting that new Hollywood recently rediscovered Murnau and Whale—in 2000, John Malkovich starred as the very weird Dracula director in *Shadow of the Vampire* and Ian

McKellen portrayed James Whale in the 1998 biopic *Gods and Monsters*, with Brendan Fraser as the straight object of his affection.

The horror comedy *The Rocky Horror Picture Show* (1975) is a great example of a queer movie that crossed over to straight audiences almost immediately. Not a horror pic per se, but a wacky homage to all haunted house/Dracula/Frankenstein movies of the past, the movie features two "innocent" newlyweds, Susan Sarandon and Barry Bostwick, who are drawn into the perverted bisexual atmosphere of the mad scientist Frank-N-Furter. "I'm just a sweet transvestite, from Transexual Transylvania," sings Tim Curry in the role. There are references to Steve Reeve movies, and Dr. Frank-N-Furter is building a "monster" who will be his sex slave—a blond gay gymrat with six-pack abs. By the end of the movie, almost everyone has engaged in sex of all kinds—heterosexual, homosexual, threesomes, etc.

Like all baby boomers coming of age in the stoned seventies, I must have seen *Rocky Horror* fifteen times. It always played at midnight after a double feature at repertory film houses. And it played on campuses all across the country. By the eighties, people sang along with *The Rocky Horror Picture Show,* talked over all the best lines, and even wore costumes from the movie. The film was probably one of the gayest influences on straight students ever to come along. And yet I must confess to another Liberace Syndrome moment: Back then, I rarely even considered the film's gay "subtext," even though the queerness there was too "out" to be subtext. *Rocky Horror* is a gay *text*—campy, swishy, and brilliant.

The Gay Event That Made Heterosexuals Sing

An amazing event is taking place in cities around the world. I first saw it in London, then in New York, then even in my hometown of Philadelphia. This event draws hopelessly heterosexual couples with their noisy children, diaper bags, and Cheerios dispensers. But it's also filled with men in nun costumes and Tyrolean dresses. I'm talking about the Singalong *Sound of Music*—if ever there was a place where gay tastes and heterosexual needs converge, this is it.

The Singalong *Sound of Music*, which began as a one-night event at the London Lesbian & Gay Film Festival, was an immediate success. Like so many kitschy gay art forms, it had no trouble crossing over to the straight world. In fact, many straight people have no idea that it was once a fairly exclusive gay event, and maybe even some gay people are confused. I was watching *Will & Grace* one night, and the writers had developed a situation in which Will was attending a *Sound of Music* sing-along in costume as Ray, a Drop of Golden Sun. In the laugh line, Grace says, "Leave it to you to gay up *The Sound of Music*." *Helloooooo. Duh*. The sing-along was "way gay" in its inception.

I spoke with Jeremy Wintroub, who works out of Chicago as the tour manager for the Sing-A-Long *Wizard of Oz*, a totally different venture than the *Sound of Music* tour but definitely inspired by it. The Sing-A-Long *Wizard of Oz* tour started in November 2002. It has played in the Hollywood

Bowl to 16,000 people, and also had a monthlong run at the Gershwin Theater in New York.

A master of ceremonies presides over the live part of the sing-along, and each audience member receives a "fun pack" with a tinsel wand, bubble mix, a noisemaker, and a kazoo. The song lyrics pop up on the bottom part of the screen. Many audience members come in costume—the costume parade is a highlight for adults and children. You're just as likely to see a gay man in drag as Glinda the Good Witch, and then next to him, a five-year-old girl in a similar getup.

Do the two audiences, straight and gay, get along?

"In most of our venues, we have a thirty percent alternative audience," said Wintroub. "We did some research and found that on the tour, our primary audience is family. But we get very positive response from both ends of the community. And the gay and family audiences get along great."

Wintroub went on to explain that the composition of the audiences can vary according to the size of the gay population in metropolitan areas. Columbus, Ohio, for example, had a big gay audience; Omaha, Nebraska, did not. And for obvious reasons, the tour sees more young family attendance for matinee performances. As we spoke, the tour was headed to the Castro Theatre in the Castroville section of San Francisco, one of America's oldest and most populated gay enclaves. "We're selling lots of block tickets for gay organizations," said Wintroub, "but we're also seeing family group sales."

The Sing-A-Long *Wizard of Oz* even has advertisements aimed at the separate target audiences, gay and straight. Says

Wintroub, "We have one featuring the Scarecrow, who says, 'Some people go both ways,' and then another that focuses on Dorothy and ruby slippers, for the kids."

What about the adult content of the stage patter that would keep gay audiences interested? "Sure, there are some double entendres," confirms Wintroub. "But it's silly stuff that goes over the kids' heads. And adult content is adult content, whether straight or gay. Like, our emcee might say to the audience, 'Now don't get jealous because I have a bigger wand.'"

The *Wizard of Oz* just might be the most American movie of all time, showing that even people from the Kansas dust bowl can dream in Technicolor. The film is absolutely wholesome and absolutely queer at the same time—no wonder straight and gay people will still pay good money to see it in the theater.

The New Gay Melodrama

The gay attraction to the homage and to historical forms of the past achieves new heights in Todd Haynes's fine film of 2002, *Far from Heaven*. I saw this film at a preview where Haynes, Julianne Moore, and Elmer Bernstein (the film's composer) appeared afterward for a discussion, months before its premiere, so I had read none of the many articles talking about what Haynes was trying to achieve. As *Far from Heaven* began, I was amazed by the manipulation of tone— the settings were so lush, the dialogue so corny, that the first few scenes made me laugh. The director seemed to be saying,

"Yeah, this is a film about the fifties—wink, wink." But then as it went on, the film made me cry. Haynes had hit the heart of what was so satisfying about the fifties melodramas (and certain soap operas)—by exaggerating life, they made it more real. It was the total gay aesthetic—pump something up, give it some artifice, and then you can finally see what it really means. *Far from Heaven* was like a movie in drag.

In the discussion afterward, Haynes talked about the films of Douglas Sirk and his gay sensibility. *Far from Heaven* was planned in homage to Sirk's film *All That Heaven Allows.*

He also spoke in minute detail about each color filter he had used to get the fifties look, and how much the costume design played a part in his vision of the movie. He launched into a five-minute discussion about how Julianne Moore's bell-shaped dresses marked her an old-fashioned, romantic woman, whereas he had dressed Patricia Clarkson, who played Julianne's best friend, in the sleeker, smoother silhouette of the future.

Queen! I thought as I listened to his elaborate analysis. I meant it as a compliment: I admire Haynes as a director, and I loved his film. It was the homosexual aesthetic in its purest form that made the movie shine. As we left the theater, my gay friend said, "Do you think straight people will get this film?" Without thinking, I said, "Yes, of course." That was the whole point. That was the miracle of this film. Haynes had crossed over—he had translated the gay sensibility for straight audiences, and had made them laugh at the bitchy daiquiri scene and then weep at the couple's agony. This was no "in" joke gay flick, like his Karen Carpenter movie starring Barbie and Ken dolls. Haynes now represents an incredible example of the gay world *improving* on straight movie artistry.

The Tradition of the Gay Leading Man

My friend Sarah and I were walking through the Hollywood Forever cemetery near my house when we came upon the headstone of the dashing leading man of the 1940s and 1950s, Tyrone Power.

"My mother loved him," said Sarah.

"Tyrone Power was gay, right?" I said.

"Yeah, people say that now. I think so. I don't think my mother ever knew that, though," said my friend.

It's true—they do say that now, and there was an entire biography focusing on Power's secret life as a homosexual. But this always leaves me feeling awkward—the man was married with children. He lived in a straight world, certainly, even if he did have homosexual proclivities.

Then we made our way over to the main mausoleum, where the great silent movie star Rudolph Valentino is buried.

"Gay," I said, looking at the floral arrangements in front of the small drawer of remains. But I wasn't talking about the flowers—I meant that Valentino was gay. At least that was always the rumor, along with the gossip that Ramón Novarro, the other great Latin-lover movie star of silents and early talkies, was homosexual.

"Yep," said Sarah.

At that moment, it struck me that so many of the actors who molded my ideas of masculinity as a little girl were either gay or bisexual.

I know I adored Montgomery Clift in *Raintree County* and *A Place in the Sun,* without even thinking about his sexuality. There was something about his dark, brooding looks that captivated me.

One night—I believe it was in 1966, when I was eleven years old—Monty appeared on the *Saturday Night at the Movies* program I loved so much, in the film *Freud.* I don't even want to think about the implications of Montgomery Clift, a repressed gay man, playing Sigmund Freud. The movie thrilled me. I couldn't stop thinking about it. Montgomery Clift saved a hysterical girl. I could learn about Freudian analysis and lust after a handsome actor at the same time.

The next day, I mentioned to my mother about how cool Montgomery Clift was. "You know, he's a homosexual," she said. No, I didn't know. And I didn't know how to feel about it. Was I supposed to be ashamed of my attraction to a gay movie star?

Why were so many of Hollywood's leading men of the past either homosexual or bisexual? And why, if you believe the rumors, are many contemporary male stars "nelly," as my gossipy gay friend words it?

Even putting aside rumors, the list of homo and bi leading men from the past is substantial: William Haines, Charles Laughton, Rudolph Valentino, Ramon Novarro, Cesar Romero, Tyrone Power, Errol Flynn, Randolph Scott, Tab Hunter, Richard Chamberlain, Raymond Burr, Sal Mineo,

James Dean, Dirk Bogarde, Anthony Perkins, Rock Hudson, Marlon Brando, John Gielgud, and, of course, Cary Grant— my beloved Cary Grant.

By the time I discovered that Cary Grant had been romantically linked to Randolph Scott and Howard Hughes, I was more worldly wise than I had been during the Montgomery Clift incident. I developed a new attitude: So what if an actor is gay? I can still fantasize about him. Of course, I was thirty when I found out that Grant was not as thoroughly heterosexual as he appeared in his movies.

Cary Grant did more to create masculinity on screen than any other actor. How ironic that he was most likely bisexual. The great love of his life was said to be fellow actor Randolph Scott, with whom he lived for seven years before embarking upon five disastrous marriages. It makes sense that Grant was discovered by the greatest cinema fag-hag of all time, Mae West. She cast him as a boy toy in *She Done Him Wrong*—it was to Grant that she uttered her famous line, "Why don't you come up and see me sometime?"

Movie critics note that Cary Grant and Katharine Hepburn were well matched in the films they did together because Hepburn's masculine traits were a good foil for Grant's softer, more feminine personality. As much as I like *Bringing Up Baby* and *The Philadelphia Story*, I think my favorite Hepburn/Grant movie is the very queer flop of a picture *Sylvia Scarlett*, directed by the gay George Cukor. Made in 1935 (five years before *The Philadelphia Story*), *Sylvia Scarlett* is the strange tale of a girl and her father who flee France to escape scandal and end up touring the English countryside as entertainers. Hepburn is dressed in men's clothing throughout most of the movie, and there is sexual tension between her and Cary Grant, who plays an insincere scallywag with a horrible cockney accent. It's almost like a chaste homosexual love affair.

Yet it is the Hitchcock version of Cary Grant that most influenced my ideal of the suave, masculine hero. I think of him dangling from Mount Rushmore in *North by Northwest*, or making love to Eva Marie Saint in the same film, especially in the final sexy scene in which the phallic train goes into the tunnel. He's also a sexy he-man in *To Catch a Thief*, captivating Grace Kelly with his bad-boy ways. No one wore a tuxedo better than Cary Grant—his Monte Carlo nightclub scenes in *To Catch a Thief* are like gorgeous male-model photo shoots.

And then there's *Notorious*, Hitchcock's thriller about patriotism and sexual attraction. The early kiss between Cary Grant and Ingrid Bergman has gone down in history as one of the sexiest in filmdom. And Grant is every girl's dream as he rescues Bergman from the clutches of her Nazi husband, Claude Rains.

By the time Stanley Donen cast him as a suave agent of many identities in the spy caper film *Charade*, Cary Grant was in his fifties, but still as handsome as ever. Costar Audrey Hepburn's androgynous look seemed to emphasize Grant's irresistible masculinity.

I don't care if Cary Grant was a nelly. He's my ideal man, and I'm sure a lot of women would agree: Homosexual or effeminate men are the closest to what heterosexual women think of as a real man, a guy with looks and brains who cares about his body and is always polite to women. That combination doesn't come along very much in the heterosexual world.

Rumors of homosexuality have swirled around many of today's leading men. Tom Cruise has sued and won over tabloid allegations that he is a homosexual. Gossip about the possible gayness of John Travolta, Brendan Fraser, Hugh Jackman, Colin Farrell, Kevin Spacey, and others will always be around. Will we ever find out who's gay and who's not? Does it matter? And, since the world of movies is all smoke and mirrors anyway, why can't filmgoers accept the idea that some leading men are bisexuals or even exclusively homosexual? I would contend that even straight leading men are following in a tradition of the gay aesthetic when it comes to "selling" male beauty.

Our culture's ideal man has always been shaped by homo vibes. As a kid I watched many Rock Hudson movies on television, and adored him as Susan Saint James's husband on TV's *McMillan & Wife*. I thought he was almost hypermasculine. In 1985, I was shocked, along with the rest of the world, to find out that he was dying of AIDS. The gossip columnist Liz Smith, who knew Hudson in the 1950s, described his appeal: "Rock was a stand-up good guy. He didn't say anything about his sexuality, but of course, we who hoped to sleep with him all speculated. I'd say it was 50-50—women and men wanted this handsome star equally."

Chapter 8

Game-Show Sissies and Gay Dads— and Was Gomer Pyle a Fairy?

Perhaps Lucy qualifies as gay television because most of the story lines typically involve Lucy masquerading as someone or something she's not in order to get into Ricky's act. Or to get more analytical, maybe Lucy appeals to gay men because on some level they can identify with Lucy and Ethel—a pair of 1950s housewives who repeatedly take delight in defying male patriarchal authority and traditional male/female gender roles.

—Stephen Tropiano,
The Prime Time Closet

TV, particularly the sitcom world, starts and ends with gay men. Until Roseanne, those gay men (and women) were much like the Jews of early Hollywood, keeping to themselves that which might turn Middle America off. Mr. Mooney, Uncle Arthur, everyone on H. R. Pufnstuf, Phyllis' unseen husband, Lars, Speed Racer, Mr. French, even real-life variety performer Alan Sues, etc., etc., etc., were all kept in the closet, however clear the subtext.

—David Poland

TV was campy from the moment it first appeared in American homes. Dad turned on the set, and the whole family watched Milton Berle prancing around in a dress. Years later, in 1999, Berle would end up suing a real estate company for six million dollars because it used an image of him dressed as Carmen Miranda in a full page ad in *Out!* magazine. The caption: "Every queen deserves a castle."

Berle declared through a lawyer that he wanted to make it clear that he had nothing against homosexuals, but he did not want anyone to think he *was* one. Berle's drag wasn't supposed to be taken seriously—it was gay, in the old-fashioned sense. "We are deeply concerned that a generation of Americans unfamiliar with Berle's classic shtick are seeing Berle depicted as a homosexual within the pages of this gay magazine," said his attorney.

Berle was ninety-one when he filed suit. Would any television viewers under the age of forty even know who he was? By the late 1990s, *Will & Grace* was already on the air, and we were all accustomed to the idea that a straight man could act gay. And Tom Hanks had done his drag time in the eighties on the campy sitcom *Bosom Buddies,* a kind of low-grade *Some Like It Hot,* or Billy Wilder Lite.

By the Lenny Bruce rule, Milton Berle *was* gay, even if he was a heterosexual. (Which all agree he was, with a penis rumored to be huge in Hollywood—who keeps these penile measurements, anyway? I thought it was mostly gay men.) Any man in a dress represents an aesthetic of artificiality. It has nothing to do with whom he screws. I don't care how married Barry Humphreys is, or how many children he's sired. His character Dame Edna is gay. Or, better than that, she is a gay icon. She is a gay diva, like Liza and Judy and Julie Newmar.

And while we're at it, another early television giant, Jack Benny, seemed gay, too, even though he was a married man. He swished, he flipped his wrists, he played the violin. The Jack Benny walk was famous—in one Lucille Ball show, as Lucy tried to seduce him, she wiggled her hips and beckoned him. "Walk this way," said Lucy. "I always do," said Jack. It was part of his onstage and on-screen character to flaunt his effeminacy. Jack Benny was a proto–Pee-wee Herman.

Proto-Gay Characters, Faux or Real

There were a lot of faux-gay men around in the early days of television. Some of them really were gay, like Wally Cox on *Mr. Peepers.* (Or was he? Some information cites Cox as a ladies' man and best friend/roommate of Marlon Brando.

Other gay websites and books claim him as a gay man and even insinuate that he was more than a roommate to Brando.)

I have a friend who's always wanted to write a book, *Pop Culture Made Me Gay*. He talks about how he lusted after Robert Conrad as James West in *Wild Wild West* and William Shatner as Captain Kirk on *Star Trek*. The camp Batman show was homoerotic to him. His favorite Monkees fantasy was Davy. No one could say these characters were intentionally gay, of course. But desire is in the eye of the beholder. If the movies are all about sex, then television is about having sex piped directly into your home.

In the sixties and seventies, even kiddie shows seemed gay, although the Liberace Syndrome saved many children and parents from realizing it. One of the local television kiddie-show hosts in Philadelphia, Gene London, used to draw, tell stories, and cry. He later went on to collect Hollywood ball gowns. Frank de Caro wrote a hilarious article in *The Advocate*, "Witchie Poo Made Me Gay," talking about how homosexual the Sid and Marty Kroft seventies show H. R. Pufnstuf really was. Even in the "innocent" late eighties, Paul Rubens was able to get away with amazing queeny scenes on *Pee-wee's Playhouse*. The homoerotic hunk, Cowboy Curtis, was played by Laurence Fishburne; I remember one funny bit in which Pee-wee mused, "Do you know what big boots mean? Big feet!"

In the sixties, seventies, and even into the eighties, most gay characters or talk-show guests were not "out." We all knew there was something different about them, especially in the way they bandied words. Game shows were a haven for queers, where wit and verbal skill could make a gay guy quotable at the dinner table.

All in the Game: Charles Nelson Reilly, Paul Lynde, and Rip Taylor

Hooray for Charles Nelson Reilly, the pipe-smoking bon vivant on *The Match Game* panel. He, along with Paul Lynde, was the only fresh voice in the ubiquitous game shows of the 1970s. And even though they and their audience denied it at the time, both were gay men.

You could always count on Chuck, in his aviator glasses and poufed hair, to liven up the boring questions with "queeny" quips and mordant observations. He was known for his flamboyant ascots and the omnipresent pipe, which in his hands looked very fey, not at all professorial.

Reilly was a Tony Award–winner for his role in *How to Succeed in Business Without Really Trying* and a denizen of the gay theater world. So what was he doing coming into America's homes? Entertaining us with wit and sarcasm that can only come from a gay perspective. During the same period, Reilly also starred in a series of enormously popular TV commercials, including the "Bic Banana Pen," in full banana-phallic regalia. (Supersize the irony, please.)

In 2001, when the gay news magazine *The Advocate* interviewed Reilly about his career, he recalled a 1970 meeting in which a certain NBC executive told him that there could be "no queers on television." At the same time, Reilly counted that he had been on the airwaves twenty-nine times in the past month. The same executive was found dead years later, murdered by a male prostitute.

Although Reilly was never exactly "out" in the sixties and seventies, he was definitely the designated homo on *The Match Game*. Before he filled out his match card, he would often fling it around or flick it with his wrist. He'd make a great show of trying to concentrate while fidgeting in his chair. Reilly often bickered with Brett Somers, a ditzy, drunken-seeming actress who would whine about her life and then taunt Reilly or complain that he was stealing her spotlight. They seemed clever and funny at the time (well, I was eleven years old!), but the Reilly/Somers exchanges seem a bit flat and dated now. One anonymous Internet fan of the game described them as an early Will and Grace, but I wouldn't go that far. Two typical clunkers from a show in 1977:

> Brett: *Boy I'm so sleepy. Before the show I took a little nippy-nap.*
> Charles: *Then you had a little nippy-nip!*
> Brett: *Don't boo me. Please don't boo me. I'm a woman in my middle years.*
> Charles: *That'll be the day!*

When *The Match Game* was scheduled into an evening slot, Reilly got bolder and began laying kisses on winning male contestants. But even before then, Reilly's gayness shone through. Another fan of the seventies show, Paul Katcher, writes on his website, "Before I knew what the term 'flaming homosexual' meant, there was Charles Nelson Reilly on my TV, filling in the following: 'I didn't have a thermometer, so I decided to take his temperature with my [BLANK].'"

One of the great things about the celebrity-driven game shows of the sixties and seventies was that the game seemed beside the point. Game shows were more discursive, filled with small jewellike narratives where gay comedians could shine. Charles Nelson Reilly was a major influence on this form, but not as large an entertainment icon as Paul Lynde, the Oscar Wilde of sitcoms and game shows. His stints on the original *The Hollywood Squares,* even if they were largely scripted, are classic examples of the gay approach to humor. Lynde could be counted on for a raunchy, liberal, snide point of view when answering host Peter Marshall's questions.

Like Reilly, Lynde was an accomplished Broadway actor who starred in *Bye Bye Birdie* on Broadway in the early sixties and in small roles in romantic comedies. Those were the days when show folks from the Big White Way still dominated the Hollywood and New York game shows. Seated in the middle square, Lynde commanded his space as thoroughly as any Shakespearean actor. His gestures—the way he used his hands and held his chin—were quite theatrical. And then there was the voice, nasal and a bit hissy. Peter Marshall, in his book about his time as host of *The Hollywood Squares,* said that Lynde received the most fan mail on the show, almost all of it from women.

Before I began writing this book, I mentioned Paul Lynde to a gay friend. "God, my grandmother *loved* Paul Lynde," he said, and then reminisced about his grandmother's favorite

Lynde comeback on *The Hollywood Squares*. I was surprised, when I looked it up, that his grandmother had quoted it perfectly:

> *Peter Marshall: Paul, why do Hell's Angels wear leather?*
> *Paul Lynde: Because chiffon wrinkles too easily.*

Can there be a gayer quote that that? You've got your leather, you've got your chiffon. And the precise way Lynde snapped out the line about it bespeaks familiarity with very feminine fabric. Yet my friend's grandmother had no idea that Paul Lynde was gay. I didn't, either, when I was a child. My parents didn't. Most of straight America didn't. It was a heavy case of the Liberace Syndrome. And yet we depended on Paul Lynde to be our bitchy clown, a role gay performers often took on in closeted days of yore.

In another exchange, Lynde skewered the mores of Bible Belt America and got away with it:

> *Peter Marshall: According to Billy Graham, is immorality contagious?*
> *Paul Lynde: I know he was down with it for about a month.*

It's not surprising that most of seventies America lacked gaydar about its homosexual game-show contestants. Even Lynde seemed confused about how to present himself. In 1971 he gave a homophobic interview to *People* magazine: "My following is straight. I'm so glad. Y'know gay people killed Judy Garland, but they're not going to kill me."

"Paul Lynde appealed to straight people because he wasn't threatening," says Nelson Aspen, exercise guru, cookbook author, and a gay TV personality in Britain and Australia. "Everyone has a gay uncle somewhere, and he was it." (At the same time Lynde was the most popular celebrity on *The Hollywood Squares,* he was also playing an effeminate warlock, Uncle Arthur, on the popular sitcom *Bewitched* [see below].)

In 1998, Bruce Vilanch, who wrote for a nighttime nineties version of *The Hollywood Squares* and became the "gay square" himself for a while, wrote a piece in *The Advocate* about how Lynde's personality opened the way for other gay and gay-sounding men on the show:

> *From then on, it was "Tillie, bar the door." Such out (or outwardly) types as Charles Nelson Reilly, Billy De Wolfe, Rip Taylor, Jim J. Bullock, Wayland Flowers and Madame, Dom DeLuise, Richard Simmons, and Jimmy Coco all found a comfortable home in one or another of the squares. Innuendo and double entendre estab-lished a permanent address at* Hollywood Squares, *and celebrities who played the gay card got the biggest—and easiest laughs.*

To watch old game shows, even those produced in eighties, is to notice a slower pace that allows ad-libbing. Games such as *To Tell the Truth, I've Got a Secret, Password, The Match Game,* and *The Hollywood Squares* were less about contestants than they were about the celebrities. These verbal-packed "contests" eventually gave way to an even chattier form, the pseudo-competitions meant to humiliate contestants, such as Chuck Barris's *The Gong Show* (1976–1980) and the apotheosis of the non–game show, *The $1.98 Beauty Show,* which debuted in 1978.

Hosted by a very gay Rip Taylor, *The $1.98 Beauty Show* was a misogynist parody with contestants of all sizes, shapes, and ages competing for a cheap crown. It was definitely a precursor to all silly reality contest shows on nowadays, such as *Fear Factor* or *Road Rules.* Rip Taylor was (and still is) a fey, mustachioed, confetti-throwing comic. As host, he elevated a very bad concept to exquisite camp. Whereas Chuck Barris was a rather brash, nasty figure on *The Gong Show,* Taylor was benignly funny.

Rip Taylor has since been grand marshal of gay parades and has spoken fairly openly about his homosexuality. Yet when I contacted his agent to interview him for this book, he declined to talk about being a gay figure on television. In addition to introducing a super-swishy homosexual image into middle America's living rooms, he is even off the charts in gay circles. On a website called "You Know You're a Queen If..." anyone who scores more than thirty points on questions is "sassier than Rip Taylor."

Recently Taylor appeared in the *Jackass* movie spawned by the popular television show. When asked why he wanted Rip Taylor to be in his movie, Johnny Knoxville said, "I love Rip Taylor. And *Jackass* has a lot of gay undertones. It's pretty much chock-full of 'em."

I guess Knoxville is right, which proves how mainstream "gay" preoccupations have become. His *Jackass* cast is forever giving one another bungee wedgies or sticking things up one another's butts.

Sky Gilbert, a gay Toronto columnist, wrote about *Jackass* in a piece called "The End of Straight." He notes that the young ensemble of buff heterosexual men is always stripping off clothes.

And what do they do after they take it all off? Well, they lick honey out of each other's ass cracks (not actually filmed in this movie, but alluded to), they stick firecrackers in each other's butts or take endless glee in having a couple of male pals over to watch them shove a dinky car toy up their rectums.

If this film holds any truth at all about what constitutes good, not-so-clean, masculine fun, well, then a lot of it must involve guys playing with each other's nasty ol' rear ends.

Queer Sitcoms, Wholesome Gay Fathers, and Queer Granddads

Among queer-studies professionals, *Bewitched* is considered the queerest sitcom ever made. This is not because of Paul Lynde's guest appearances as Samantha's "queeny" Uncle Arthur, nor because of Agnes Moorehead's presence as Samantha's mother. (Moorehead has widely been alleged to have been a lesbian, despite two marriages.) And although Dick Sargent, the second man to play Samantha's husband, Darrin, later came out after the show went off the air, even that is not why *Bewitched* has been dubbed a gay show.

No, the queer designation comes about more on metaphorical terms. Samantha, a witch by birth, has decided to marry a mortal. She promises husband Darrin that she will not reveal her true identity to anyone else, and that she will not practice witchcraft in her daily life. So Samantha becomes a closeted witch, who can only share her true lifestyle with her extended witch family when they drop by to create havoc. The term "witch hunt" has always been used in modern times to mean unfair prejudice. And here, in the modern tale of Samantha Stephens in 1964 America, we have a story that can appeal to anyone who feels squelched by "normal" society.

I loved the show as a kid, and felt it unfair that Samantha had to do things the tedious mortal way. I would never vacuum a house if I were a witch, I vowed to my nine-year-old self. I adored Samantha and hated Darrin with the same ferocity that I hated "Master," the piggy astronaut in *I Dream of Jeannie,* who always locked his female genie in a bottle. (Talk about campiness!) It turns out that a lot of gay boys were also watching *Bewitched,* and that they saw Samantha's plight as similar to their own. Samantha had her "straight" life and the "witch life" in which she could summon William Shakespeare to her side, or fly up to the North Pole to see Santa Claus. All of her relatives were flamboyant and fun. All of Darrin's associates were straight and dull.

Early television sitcoms fall into two categories. Either the writers presented a utopian idea of what the American family should be (*Leave It to Beaver, Father Knows Best*) or they gave us a means to escape into a fantasy of otherness. I preferred shows in the second *Bewitched*-type category, such as *My Mother the Car*, in which Jerry Van Dyke bought a used car only to find that it was inhabited by his mother's spirit (the voice of Ann Sothern), or *My Living Doll*, where Julie Newmar played a beautiful six-foot robot girl. Is it just a coincidence that Ann Sothern and Julie Newmar are both idolized by many gay men?

The later *Mork & Mindy* had the same campy tone—when aliens come to town, it's always time to hike up the campiness. The scenes in which the aliens reverted to their natural selves always played as humans putting on alien "drag" costumes— Uncle Martin in his shiny green suit with the antennae visible on his head, and Mork in his spacesuit, holding a helmet and talking to his planet's commanders.

Thinking back on it now, these fantasy sitcoms seem as queer as that great gay film favorite *The Wizard of Oz*, which was telecast yearly from the 1960s on. (Although it was made for the movie screen, few Americans under seventy have ever seen it in a theater.) *The Wizard of Oz* has been dissected again and again as a quintessentially queer movie. Yet it is the most important pop-culture nexus between the straight and gay worlds.

Television homosexuality would be easier to write about if every actor rumored to be gay suddenly admitted to it. But the fact remains that Gomer Pyle (Jim Nabors) *might* have been gay (don't ask, don't tell). Mr. Nabors isn't saying. And

Mr. Brady (Robert Reed) of *The Brady Bunch* really *was* homosexual, by his own later admission. Perhaps that's why he came across as so gentle and kind. One of the big revelations for me was Grandpa Walton—in real life, Will Geer had lived with the founder of an early homosexual organization, The Mattachine Society. Grandpa Walton was a communist *and* a homo. I love that. One of my gay friends in West Hollywood told me a story about Will Geer's later years, when he lived in the Hollywood Hills and still admired handsome young men. "I might be too old to cut the mustard, but I can still lick the jar," he was supposed to have said on many occasions.

Gay Writers, Straight Shows

"The show was a fantasy world of beach parties, sideburns, and little black dresses, and I, for two blessed hours, got to forget about being a gay teenager," reminisced Aaron Harberts in a magazine piece when *Beverly Hills, 90210* was about to go off the air. Harberts and his writing partner, Gretchen Berg, became part of the writing staff for *90210*'s last two seasons. "Some say that *90210* has had a profound effect on gay culture and vice versa. . . . Before *Friends* and *Frasier*, before gay and lesbian characters were simply plot-point twists or quirky best friends, *90210* tackled many topics important to gay people. We did coming out in high school, gay adoption, and gay bashing."

Harberts says he and his writing partner also were able to "flex our high-camp muscles" by creating Gina, the spiteful, figure-skating cousin character. "The problem with camp, though," writes Harberts, "is its ultimate soullessness, and our show was anything but soulless."

Is there a gay sensibility among television writers that makes their scripts different, even when they are writing about straight characters? "Yes and no," says Philip Gerson, who has written for *Murder, She Wrote, Christy,* and *Dr. Quinn, Medicine Woman.* I spoke to him at an OTF (Out in Theater and Film) benefit in Hollywood.

"I'm Jewish and gay," says Gerson. "Both factors contribute to an outsider experience, especially when working on shows with Christian backgrounds and themes. And writing a television show is very much a team effort. It's all about putting out slices of bread, and the bread has to be pretty much the same from week to week. There has to be a consistent voice, but occasionally you can slip things in."

Pressed further, Gerson says he can remember a few specific instances in which his homosexuality influenced his scripts. He believes that there is a gay sense of humor that can show up even on dramatic shows. In terms of content, though, he cites two *Dr. Quinn* episodes. "One of them wasn't my idea, but I worked on it. Christine Berardo, another writer, had discovered that Walt Whitman visited Colorado Springs during one of the years the show took place. So there was an episode that portrayed him reading and teaching poetry and meeting up with his male partner while he took a rest cure in Colorado Springs. Dr. Quinn even had to confront her own homophobia as her adopted son became close to Whitman."

"Another episode I wrote," continued Gerson, "was specifically a metaphor for AIDS. I told the other writers that I was approaching it that way. It involved a woman who had leprosy. She came to visit the town and no one knew what she had, but after they saw her leprosy, they shunned her. Remember, I was writing about 1872, so it was pre–germ theory. It fit the AIDS model perfectly. It captured the type of fear that was around in the 1980s, before we knew what was going on."

Big Numbers, Envelopes, and Snow White

The stylishness on all those 70s variety shows, seen as Hollywood glamour, was not just glamorous; it had a gay sensibility.

—Stephen Troppiano

Variety shows and awards ceremonies have always been the television formats that most resemble parties. Not surprisingly, gay men have made major contributions.

Once, when I was writing a spoof of *Gone with the Wind*, I decided to canvass people and ask them what they remember about the original book or movie. I was very surprised that the one *Gone with the Wind* moment most people remembered best was not from the movie. It was the famous Carol Burnett sketch in which she comes down a grand staircase as Scarlett O'Hara, dressed in a ball gown made of curtains. Yet there's one difference: Burnett's Scarlett is wearing a dress that *still has the curtain rods in it*. The jerry-rigged garment makes her look huge. The effect is hilarious as Burnett tries to move from side to side with large metal rods inhibiting her motion.

I'd never thought of where the idea came from until I saw Carol Burnett interviewed for a Bob Mackie tribute. Mackie is the talented gay designer who is famous for his over-the-top Oscar gowns, especially those worn by Cher. He also dressed Cher in her outrageous dresses for *The Sonny and Cher Show*. Burnett said that she was struggling with what her curtain dress should look like. She knew that she wanted it to be "over the top," but how? Bob Mackie suddenly blurted out the curtain rod idea, and a classic sketch moment was born.

Viewing the sketch recently, I was struck by how much Burnett looked like a drag queen at the top of the stairs. It was a moment that would have played well in a dingy gay bar, but which also worked great in a prime-time television show in the 1970s. *Gone with the Wind*, like *The Wizard of Oz*, was one of the last great films that went into our culture as both straight and gay camp.

I wonder if most of straight America realizes that most award shows are very gay. The reign of gay writer Bruce Vilanch at the Academy Awards ushered in a new level of savage wit. Where else would you get a shot of Judi Dench with the voiceover "This thong is killing me." One year, after Dr. Laura's homophobic remarks, Vilanch wrote some scathing lines for Billy Crystal, about how Dr. Laura had wanted to come to the ceremony, but couldn't find anyone who would do her hair. The joke was slow to build, since it hinged on knowing that most hairdressers in Hollywood (or anywhere) are gay.

The gayest Academy Awards ever was possibly the most controversial one, in 1992, when Rob Lowe danced to "Proud Mary" with a live costumed actress playing Disney's Snow White. It was a horrible, laughable moment, produced by Allan Carr, the producer of the film *Grease* and the lamentable Village People movie *Can't Stop the Music*. Carr was "out" before most people knew what "out" was, and he's a fascinating peripheral character in Hollywood history. The manager of Ann-Margret and other diva celebrities, Carr wore bizarre caftans and was famous for his parties—he gave one in a former maximum-security jail, where he locked up Truman Capote and other celebrities.

Straight Sitcoms That Are Very Gay

In 2003, *Vanity Fair* did a cover article on gay television, with pictures of the actors from *Queer as Folk, Queer Eye for the Straight Guy,* and *Will & Grace*. Yet the inside story claimed that the gayest sitcom ever was *Friends*, with its emphasis on male companionship and Gen-X friends-over-family relationships.

Although the old-fashioned sitcom was family-based, it's true that the more successful shows of the recent past have been work-based or set among a larger group of friends. *Frasier*, because of the closeness and effeminacy of the two brothers, Miles and Frasier Crane, does seem "gay," and one episode finally even confronted that notion, with Patrick Stewart playing an impresario with a crush on Frasier. *Frasier* also boasts a wonderful writing staff, including several gay writers.

The cocreator of *Friends*, David Crane, is gay, but he does not easily acknowledge the show's gay sensibility in interviews. What I've always liked about *Friends* is the easy banter among the characters about the gayness that is in all of us. The female and male characters frequently find themselves in potentially homoerotic situations and get out of them not without a tinge of regret. The show is about intimacy, whether it is achieved via friendship or sex. And it is also about appearance vs. reality. Time and again, the characters puzzle over Chandler's apparent gayness, or what makes him appear gay to others. All the while, they accept him and accept their own rather fluid sexual attractions to the guest characters who stop in weekly.

"The gayest episode of *Friends*," says Daniel Coleridge, an openly gay young critic for *TV Guide*, "is 'The One with the Nap.' Joey and Ross fall asleep on the couch in each other's arms. It's so intimate, so refreshing. And both of them admit afterwards that it's the best nap they've ever had. I found it sweet—both men were vulnerable. It was sexy in a way, without any sex."

Coda: The Inevitable *Will & Grace*

And then there's *Will & Grace*. One can't talk about gay television without mentioning it.

This popular sitcom, which features two gay male charac-

ters in prominent roles, is the one vehicle that has success-
fully brought gay-straight relationships into America's living
rooms. Yes, it's somewhat trite and stereotypical. Yet with all
of its jokes about superior gay design and taste, the show is
constantly highlighting the homosexual contribution to sophisticated living.

Of course Will and Jack, the two gay characters on the
show, are not "real" gay people, any more than the straight
characters on *Friends* are realistically drawn (how many hard-
working people in their mid-thirties do you know who constantly visit one another on a weeknight?). But, ironically, the
relationship between Will, a gay man, and Grace, a straight
woman, borders on every woman's fantasy. Will is handsome,
witty, and attentive. He is a dream man in the same way that
Rock Hudson, Cary Grant, and Montgomery Clift were, but
Will is "out," and sexually unavailable to Grace. The yearning so many women felt for the homosexual leading men of
years gone by has finally been brought out of the closet.

Add to this the strangeness of Will being played by a
straight man, Eric McCormack, and we have completed the
cultural circle. In the three decades after World War II, the
perfect man was virile and "straight," and played by a homosexual. In the last decade, that man is sensitive and "gay,"
played by a heterosexual.

Chapter 9

Music:
Play That
Funky Music,
Gay Boy!

It was fascinating, from the sixties onwards, to see how often gays and their lifestyle had cropped up in the history of British music business. . . . In one form or another, the influence of gays on the British [music] industry has been on a par with the influence of blacks and black music on the American industry.

—from a webpage about the British music
industry in the early 1970s

Tutti Frutti, aw rootie,
A-wop-bop-a-loo-bop-a-lop-bam-boom
—"Tutti Frutti," by Little Richard

Disco music was for dancing, disco was for having a good time, and gay people, who had been prevented from dancing together in virtually all the bars across the United States until the very late years of the 1960s (or in some cases in the 1970s), embraced it and were liberated by it.

—from an Internet essay: "Disco Music Is Gay Music"

Rock and roll was invented by blacks and homosexuals in the 1950s, and then the two cultures converged once again in the late 1960s to bring disco to American dance floors.

Conservative commentators and fundamentalist preachers in the 1950s and 1960s protested that rock and roll was all about sex. They were right. The very name—rock and roll—was slang for sexual intercourse. Rock and roll liberated, once and forever, the pelvis from the rest of the body. Rock and roll is high-speed, raucous narcissism. Rock and roll is an exuberant marginal art form that started out black and gay, and within a few years had become the number-one obsession of heterosexual teenagers all over the world.

For me, there were two seminal moments in gay/straight rock and roll history: September 9, 1956, when television censors ordered that Elvis's moving hips were not to be seen on *The Ed Sullivan Show,* and January 1956, when Pat Boone recorded Little Richard's provocative tune, "Tutti Frutti."

Pat Boone was the antithesis of Elvis. Pat wore nice sports

jackets and white buck shoes, and his hips did not move. And compared to Pat Boone, Little Richard was the Antichrist. Could they have chosen anyone straighter or whiter to record "Tutti Frutti," Little Richard's flamboyant ode to sex? Little Richard wore pancake makeup and lipstick. He called himself "The king of rock and roll—and the queen, too!" America wasn't ready for his queerness, but they loved his music.

If we trace the gay influence on rock music in America, all roads lead to Little Richard, who had an enormous influence on Jerry Lee Lewis, Elvis, the Beatles, and even the Rolling Stones. He's the queer godfather of flamboyant rock and roll.

"His image was an immaculate conception," wrote *Rolling Stone* magazine about Little Richard, "a fantasy born of years in traveling medicine shows, drag-queen revues, churches and clubs. . . . But in Fifties America, this made for a terrible mess. He was black and gay, talented and loud. . . ."

The Boone cover of "Tutti Frutti" is a heterosexual anthem to nothingness, almost a case study in what happens when you rob a vital art form of its most original ingredients. With the bland Boone behind the microphone, the rewritten song rose to the top of the charts almost immediately. It was an instant crossover, a complete gay-to-straight conversion.

To look at the history of popular music is to see that constant gay-straight-gay cycle that seems to run through all entertainment forms. Gay men have always had an enormous influence on the music straight people love. I've found it peculiar to discover a gay presence in music forms I considered hopelessly heterosexual, such as heavy metal and rap.

But before we get to that, I'd like to pause for a flashback, to pray at the altar of the gay man who most influenced straight people's musical tastes before the advent of rock and roll, Cole Porter.

The Church of Cole Porter: The Queer Supremacy of Show Tunes

If a guy likes show music, he's got to be gay, right? Not always, of course. But in recent years it's become a cultural joke because show music, like opera, is a much older form of music than rock and roll, and those who enjoy it are necessarily a bit alienated from the mainstream rock music scene. I know that when I go to cabaret shows featuring the tunes of Cole Porter, George Gershwin, Irving Berlin, Johnny Mercer, or Duke Ellington, I meet only two types: gay male couples (of any age) or elderly heterosexual couples.

Yet during the heyday of show music, before and after World War II, it was mostly young heterosexual couples who enjoyed these tunes, dancing and courting to the love ballads that came from Broadway musicals. They didn't realize that many of them had been written by gay men. Cole Porter, in particular, wrote love ballads that were made for romance; most were later recorded by super-straight artists. Frank Sinatra's Cole Porter album is a classic example. How many heterosexuals fell in love to Porter's clever songs, which vibrated with a flamboyant, erotic essence that so reflected the gay sensibility? How many brides danced to "Begin the Beguine" or

"Night and Day" at their wedding receptions? Because Porter wrote the lyrics as well as the melodies, they are love songs replete with a wicked sense of humor and mature sexual content.

In "I Get a Kick out of You," from the show *Anything Goes,* Porter's lyrics compare the love object to cocaine, alcohol, and an airplane ride. "I get no kick from cocaine/Mere alcohol doesn't thrill me at all . . ." His song "Always True to You, Darling, in My Fashion" is an ode to casual adultery motivated by monetary gain, as is another, "My Heart Belongs to Daddy," in which a young woman explains that she loves a young man, but also loves the gifts and money bestowed upon her by her rich sugar daddy.

In his lyrics, Porter is always juxtaposing hard sexual facts with lovely, soaring melodies. His is a very gay sensibility. His haunting song "After You" focuses on the end of an affair even as it is just beginning. "It Was Just One of Those Things" is an upbeat, sassy song about an ill-fated one-night stand; "It's Alright with Me" is an honest exploration of "revenge sex," in which the singer/narrator of the song agrees that he or she will have sex with someone, even "though your lips are tempting, they're the wrong lips . . ."

Compare Porter's gay sensibility to Irving Berlin's more straight-and-narrow approach to romance. Berlin's most engaging love ballad is "Always," a sweet song with very simple lyrics: "I'll be loving you Always/With a love that's true Always." Though Berlin did write extremely clever songs, witty lyrics never made it into his love ballads. They were, to put it mildly, sappy. But Porter managed to inject drama and eroticism into his love songs. "Night and Day," for example, is

MUSIC

169

oozing with physical references to sex: "Night and day under the hide of me / There's an oh, such a hungry yearning burning inside of me / and its torment won't be through / Till you let me spend my life making love to you . . ."

Porter's songs are steamy. There is never any sexual coyness. He knew the purpose of a love song was to get someone into bed. If we fast-forward ourselves, we can understand the vast difference between Porter's blatant eroticism and Irving Berlin's staid romanticism by comparing, say, the Beatles' "Why Don't We Do It in the Road?" to the Association's "Cherish."

I love homosexual love songs. Most of America does, although they don't know that they are queer songs. And who knows, really, to whom a love song has been written? I've come across several sources who claim that Noel Coward's "Mad About the Boy" was written about Cary Grant. Noel Coward, who never hid his homosexuality from anyone, still declined to declare himself officially gay. It wasn't his style, and he was often quoted as saying that he would admit it, but he was afraid to frighten the little old ladies. According to William McBrien, the most recent biographer of Cole Porter, many of his most poignant love songs were written late at night when he would also write letters to gay lovers far away. How many heterosexual couples have danced to melodies and words written for gay males?

The sexiest love song in the world is Rodgers and Hart's "Bewitched, Bothered and Bewildered." In the show *Pal Joey*, it's sung by a woman of the world who's fallen head over heels with a scoundrel, a man she knows is probably not even faithful to her. The lyrics, created by Lorenz Hart, a tormented, closeted gay man, carry a palpable sense of longing I've seldom seen expressed, and include sultry lines alluding to wild nights: "Vexed again/Perplexed again/Thank God I can be oversexed again." The singer admits that her man is not much for conversation, "but horizontally speaking, he's at his very best . . ." There's a refreshingly wicked gayness to that line.

Shades of Gay: Early Rock and Queerdom

Yes, we've all heard that Brian Epstein, the Beatles' manager, was gay. Blah, blah, blah. And we've also heard the rumors that Epstein and John Lennon were lovers on a 1963 vacation trip to Spain. (There's even a movie based on that conjecture, *The Hours and the Times*.) Blah, blah again. Did Lennon write "You've Got to Hide Your Love Away" for Epstein? Does it matter? The Rolling Stones' first manager was gay, too, so it would be tempting to say that there was a gay mafia in early rock, but that would be stretching things a bit too far.

Some of the queer context of early rock and roll is impossible to pin down. Rock was always, after all, sexually omnivorous. And the early look was androgynous. Unisex was in. It's hard to remember how shocking it was to see young men with long hair in 1963. And certainly someone like Brian Epstein, who painstakingly created the Beatles' look of matching suits and mod haircuts, can be credited with spoon-feeding a gay fashion sense to the heterosexual masses. But so did Rudi Gernreich, the gay inventor of the topless bathing suit.

Gayness in the early rock music scene was difficult to distinguish from the general joy of sexual perversity in the 1960s. The art world, with David Hockney, Robert Rauschenberg, and Andy Warhol, was far ahead of the music world in developing and honing its gay sensibility.

In looking at the reactions of a largely straight American audience, there was one major factor going on during the rock-and-roll revolution: denial. Americans were fairly oblivious to gayness as a whole—even some closeted gay people, it seems. Times were different then, as older folks like to say. But they really were.

America *had* to ignore the influences of rock music. It stood for everything un-American: sex, drugs, and a healthy disrespect for authority. Similarly, kids went crazy for the campy, gayish stage antics of Mick Jagger of the Rolling Stones and Ray Davies of the Kinks. They were subversive; they were "queer," even if they were straight. Most of the action in any rock concert concentrated on the mouth and the crotch. In fact, by the Lenny Bruce rule, all male rock stars were essentially homosexual, even if they slept with women.

Pete Townsend of The Who caused a stir when he was "outed" as a bisexual. Yet gender-bending and homosexual motifs had always been a significant part of his songwriting. "I've written eleven songs with 'boy' in the title," Townsend once said in stage patter, talking to an audience during a solo show. One of them, "Rough Boys," has explicit gay vibes: "Rough boys/Don't walk away/I wanna buy you leather." He told *Playboy* magazine that he had agreed in an interview that it was a song about gay boys, and that the press had then jumped to dub him bisexual, even though he had never said he was. Again, does it matter? "Rough Boys" is a great rock song with a gay sensibility. So what if it was written by a man who defines himself as straight?

It's doubtful that the many straight fans of The Who ever thought of Pete Townsend as potentially queer or even queer-friendly in the seventies and eighties, although much homophobia erupted when he was arrested in January 2003, charged with owning child pornography. (Townsend, who claimed he was researching an idea he had that he was abused as a child, was set free on bail, and no charges were filed.) The Who, like the Stones and later glamrock and heavy-metal bands, put on a really good show, filled with high-voltage queer theatricality. *Tommy,* their rock opera, is a good example of an essentially effeminate form (rock) revamped as a macho-queer extravaganza.

Another sexually ambiguous guy is Ray Davies of the Kinks, who's never talked about what he does under the covers. The Kinks' biggest hit was "You Really Got Me," but the group has passed into gay rock history for the sly, clever novelty song "Lola," which is rumored to have been based on a real incident that occurred in Ray Davies's life.

The narrator of "Lola" meets a beautiful woman in a bar and goes home with her, only to discover that she is a transvestite. It's a cheeky, fun song that appeals to all sorts of audiences, with a frisson at the end that leads the listener to believe that the guy slept with Lola anyway.

Or at least that's what I always thought. That's before, in looking around the Web, I encountered a hapless victim of the

Liberace Syndrome who seemed to have no feel for gay themes. This was a poor fellow with the apt screen name "Pee-brain," a hopelessly heterosexual male Kinks fan who wrote a plaintive posting on a Kinks fan site about the song "Lola." He was in deep denial, it seems, about the song's final lyrics: "Well I'm not the world's most masculine man/but I know what I am, and that I'm a man/so is Lola." I don't think I've ever read a funnier stream-of-consciousness epiphany:

Now that [last line] *can be looked at 2 different ways. Lola is glad he's a man because he gave her a good time that night with his manness.*

 or

Lola is also a man . . . Now why I never saw that other meaning until now . . . beats me . . . but no . . . no i dont like it . . . that's scary . . . cause I use to repeatedly listen to this song thinking about this babe I met at a retreat who was very sexy but talked in a low voice like a man hahaha hillarious . . . but there's no way she was a man . . . way too fine a girl for that. but anyways. There should be a warning label on gay songs like this like "Warning: This song is gay."

Dave Davies, Ray's brother and fellow Kinks member, was asked about the whole issue of the Kinks' gayness in a Trouser Press interview in 1979. "When we first came over here [to the States] all the people who came backstage were all guys," he told Eliott Cohen. "Other bands used to attract female groupies, but we would only get guys—gay guys, straight guys. A lot of people used to comment how amusing it was to see so many guys backstage after a gig."

Noting that "part of Ray's personality is to act campy," Dave Davies wondered why so many people wanted to categorize Ray as a homosexual. The campiness, he said, was "just an expression of what he is; I don't think it has anything to do with whether he's actually gay or not."

Gay or not, we should all thank Ray Davies for his contributions to a genre rare in rock music. In movies and onstage, transvestites and drag queens are a dime a dozen. It's rarer to find a lusty, funny rock anthem to sexy guys in dresses.

Groin Control to Major Tom: The Father of Glam Rock, David Bowie

In the family tree of rock, as I said, many singers seem to descend from Little Richard. David Bowie could have been formed out of his rib. Both artists are enthusiastic transvestites and flamboyant performers. The amazing difference between them, and the reason that Bowie has gone on to deeply influence the course of rock performance, perhaps more than anyone else, is that *Bowie was actually marketed as a homosexual!*

Bowie's manager, Tony Defries, perhaps with the input of Bowie's wife at the time, Angela Barnett, decided that having the creator of Ziggy Stardust declared gay would increase the fascination with his act, thereby spurring album sales. Anecdotal evidence suggests that Bowie went along with this marketing decision even though he felt uncomfortable. In January 1972, he gave an interview to *Melody Maker* magazine, declaring that he was gay and always had been.

It was the homo shot heard 'round the world.

Later Bowie would disavow those comments, saying that the interview with the magazine had been the worst decision in his life. He gave an interview to *Playboy* in 1976 declaring himself bisexual, and later realigned himself as heterosexual in a cover story in *Rolling Stone*. The homosexual rumors abound still, especially since his ex-wife wrote in her 1993 memoir *Backstage Passes* that she had once found Bowie and Mick Jagger in bed together. Most reliable sources say that this "tell-all" piece of trivia is false.

Yet, again, do we need the anatomical details here? Whatever his sexuality, Bowie is a major gay icon who has influenced straight rock and roll and has long been accepted by straight audiences. It's ironic that Bowie seems to have traveled the exact opposite path of most queer rock artists. Instead of a journey from the closet out into the gay world, he started as gay and got straighter as the years went on. And yet, as a consequence of boldly outing himself, the proverbial closet door could never open up and swallow him, however heterosexual he wanted to be. He remained out there as a queer artist.

Thirty years ahead of his time, Bowie made being gay *hip*.

Whatever sexual confusions might have swirled around him during his long career, Bowie is frankly in debt to gay artists of the past. His background in mime helped him create his exotic characters, such as Ziggy Stardust and the Thin White Duke. And his love of cabaret compositions, among them the songs of the Parisian songwriter Jacques Brel, shows in his intricate lyrics and sophisticated song concepts. Perhaps that's why his performance work seems so gay. In a 1998 *Legends* interview, Bowie acknowledged the gay influences on his music. In 1960s London, he said, "[a] lot of straight guys would go to the gay clubs because of the kind of music they played. They played much better music than most clubs had."

In an early comment to the press, Bowie's manager Defries said that he saw Bowie as "a Marlon Brando or a James Dean–type star. I see him more in that category of larger-scale untouchable." It's interesting that he would compare him to two of the world's greatest sexually ambiguous movie-star icons.

Bowie = gay = hip. It's surprising how, nowadays, so many straight performers will come right out and say it: They wish they were gay. Nirvana's Kurt Cobain said it, and wrote about it in his diaries. Momus (aka Nicholas Currie), the British cult singer, gave an interview to the *Scottish Gay Times* in which he talked about how much he admires the gay sense of alienation, and how he regrets being straight. Momus referenced Bowie and other glam rockers as the greatest influences on his generation.

> *I went to boarding school and we were all into Glamrock and at twelve everybody at school was in bed with some-body else in the dorm: it was that big latency period. We were all listening to David Bowie and Lou Reed and Marc Bolan, and convinced we were gay ourselves, and that that was a good thing to be.*

Bowie shows up as an influence in many contemporary rockers' comments to the press. Not surprisingly, queer performers such as Marilyn Manson glorify him, yet other mainstream groups such as Radiohead also pay him homage. "I just admire David Bowie in the 70's," says Radiohead's Ed O'Brien. "Sometimes he brought out two albums a year. He was on a mission. His albums were hit and miss sometimes, but he was brilliant because of that."

With a career that has encompassed glamrock, punk, and R&B, and even movie acting roles, Bowie still has a firm hold on more than one generation of fans. When I asked a thirty-five-year-old friend about Bowie, he gushed about how he was the one star who made him feel it was okay to be gay, and recalled the cosmic experience of seeing Bowie live for the first time:

I was about twelve years old when he came to Philly on his Serious Moonlight tour. I was young and kind of small, so I got swept away in the sea of people rushing for their seats and the stage. I didn't know where I was heading. Bowie was already into his second song, "Heroes," when the sea of people parted and I found myself in the front row, staring practically face to face with David Bowie.

I felt the same way about it as people who claim to see angels or the Virgin Mary. Bowie seemed more otherworldly than human, blindingly bright. His hair was platinum blond and he wore a canary yellow suit. I was hooked from that moment on.

Disco Music, a Gay American Art Form

If you need evidence that gay dance-music culture has forever influenced straight America, just stop by any wedding reception to watch grandmothers perform the Village People's disco hit "Y.M.C.A." while gyrating suggestively. After my mother enjoyed herself dancing to that tune at my fortieth birthday party, I asked her if she thought of it as gay. Her reply was a blank stare.

I shouldn't be so snooty. I was in high school in the seventies; the idea that disco was gay never crossed our minds, although I did notice that a few of my effeminate male friends enjoyed dancing to it more than others. (Ah, the stereotype of the terrific gay dancer. Roseanne Barr once said, "Thank god for gay men. Without them, fat women would have no one to dance with.")

In the late seventies, straight people took to disco like ducks to water. But that was a kind of death knell for the form. Soon the disco craze resulted in crossover movies such as *Saturday Night Fever* (1977), which spawned a polyester tight-suit fashion look that was decidedly gay yet was sported by millions of straight guys on dance-club dates all across America. The Bee Gees' soundtrack for the movie dominated America's airwaves and sold millions of copies. Yet the incredible disco cycle—from straight to gay to straight again—remained fairly hidden. The majority of heterosexual disco fans never knew that the form was virtually invented by a gay man—or, I should say, "adapted."

In the late 1960s, gay bars began playing almost exclusively black soul music and rhythm and blues. In 1971, a former male model, Tom Moulton, was vacationing on Fire Island when he went to a bar and noticed that the black music playing didn't last long enough for the dancers to enjoy the dance. Seeing that the dancers were frustrated by the three-minute running time of the songs, Moulton created the first disco mix tape, which featured a DJ instrumental break and a blended, longer running time. His disco mixes became an industry standard, and he is credited with inventing the twelve-inch disco record essential to the dance club throughout the seventies.

Perhaps the campiest gay disco act to worm its way into the straight world was The Village People. The group was created by producer Jacques Morali, who scouted Greenwich Village dance clubs and Broadway shows to develop a group that contained virtually every gay icon of the time, although they were officially described as being "from various American social groups." There was the fireman, the policeman, the motorcycle driver, the mustachioed leatherman, and the Indian chief. Astoundingly, the Village People had such crossover appeal, many heterosexuals never caught on that they were gay. Or never wanted to. Call it the classic Liberace Syndrome. Along with "Y.M.C.A.," their hits included the heavily ironic "In the Navy" and "Macho Man." It's hard to remember that the words "macho" and "machismo" had been little used popularly until the 1980s. Suddenly everyone talked about being macho. It's interesting to think that a group of gay singers gave new vocabulary to a world where "manly men" were running around not eating quiche and generally having a good time bashing feminists during the conservative Reagan period.

Bubblegum Tunes, Big Diva Dreams, and Boys, Boys, Boys

Top-twenty tunes with major radio airplay keep the music industry alive. And when it comes to insipid songs that stick in your head forever, gay men are *there*.

"I don't know why, but we've always loved bubblegum music," says my friend Frank, who was a DJ for years. "Even I'm embarrassed that gay friends in their forties are buying Clay Aiken's albums and listening to Britney and Christina. I have one friend who actually likes Kelly Clarkson."

Gay men have always had their fingers on the pulse of teenybopper desires. They've played a role in creating and then worshipping rock divas. But no one knows quite why some singers and groups have gay appeal and others don't.

There is a long line of gay songwriters and performers who produced make-out and dance music for teenagers from the fifties on. Johnny Mathis, long closeted but now openly gay, was the symbol of the romantic crooner into the seventies. In the nostalgic Barry Levinson film *Diner*, Eddie Simmons asks the eternal question: Do his friends prefer to make out with their girlfriends to Mathis or Sinatra?

Barry Manilow, still closeted, was another sexually ambiguous seventies crooner with a huge gay and straight following. He got his start as Bette Midler's accompanist at the gay baths in New York and San Francisco. His hits include the bubblegummy "Copacabana," "Mandy," and "I Can't Smile Without You."

And then there is the Australian Peter Allen, who has been immortalized by Hugh Jackman in the new musical *The Boy from Oz*. Just by virtue of having worked with Judy Garland and having been married briefly to her daughter, Liza Minnelli, Allen could qualify as the gayest pop star in history. His catchy hit "I Go to Rio" embodies the gay joie de vivre, yet it caused toe tapping in straight circles across America. His wonderfully campy torch song "Don't Cry Out Loud" has become a standard for diva performance.

Elton John, long before he was out of the closet, and well before he became a Disney composer, produced beautiful love songs for heterosexuals ("Your Song") and action tunes about lonely astronauts ("Rocket Man"). He has been the King of Pop since the 1970s; it was interesting to watch how his relationship with his personal diva, Princess Diana, created a macabre opportunity to rewrite his song (written with Bernie Taupin) "Candle in the Wind" for her funeral ceremony in 1997. The amazing amount of radio airplay provided to the funeral version of that song represents a watershed moment in which the straight world acknowledged the cathartic power of a good old-fashioned queer tune.

Last but not least in the hit parade come George Michael and Boy George, who rode the MTV airwaves as pop supremacists for a number of years in the 1980s. Both were gay and closeted; both became spectacularly undone for a while after their sexuality and drug habits were revealed. Boy George is now the consummate disc jockey, after recovering from the disaster of his Broadway debut in *Taboo*. Rosie O'Donnell supposedly couldn't figure out why *Taboo* didn't sell tickets, but I saw the show, and I don't think matinee ladies are quite ready for a big song-and-dance number about casual sex set in a male urinal.

Top-40 music has always been driven by female pop divas in a tradition that goes back to Judy Garland, Rosemary Clooney, Peggy Lee, Aretha Franklin, Petula Clark, Leslie Gore, and Dusty Springfield. Gay men are the biggest supporters of past and present divas. Eventually, anyone who becomes a diva for gay audiences loses her last name, a phenomenon that has spread to influence the way heterosexual audiences refer to female singers. Divas are so big that they need no surnames—there are Tina, Cyndi, Belinda, Brittany, Christina, Bette, Barbra, and, of course, Madonna and Cher, who got rid of their last names before they even got into show business.

In the last ten years, the popular divas have acknowledged their gay followings as well as their gay influences. Cher, who made an amazing comeback with the song "Believe" in 1998, talks often about the debt she owes to her gay audiences.

"I did 'Strong Enough' specifically for my gay fans," Cher told a music reporter, referring to her 1999 hit single. "I did a gay version on the spot, because I thought this would be such a cool thing to do. My gay fans have been so loyal and so great, at times when other fans weren't there. Gay fans usually love you when you're in the dumps, in the toilet, they're still there for you. I have a very Judy Garland feeling."

Madonna is another pop superstar who brought a particularly gay sensibility to the pop scene. As divas go, she's at the top of the heap. After she announced her Re-Invention tour in the winter of 2004, nearly every gay man I know rushed to get tickets. The bad movies Madonna makes—*The Next Best Thing* and the remake of *Swept Away*—do nothing to dim her gay fans' ardor. In several interviews, Madonna has praised her Michigan high-school ballet teacher, who helped her appreciate the finer things in life and brought her out to gay dance clubs. "I feel like I'm always working with gay men," she told Don Shewey. "For some reason that's who I have the most camaraderie with. I don't really know why. I think, on the one hand, I feel their persecution. They are looked at as outsiders, so I relate to that."

Madonna introduced the gay dance the "Vogue" to straight audiences. Her huge hits such as "Like a Virgin" and "Material Girl" were on the lips of gay men, prepubescent girls, and straight couples everywhere during the 1980s and early 1990s. Madonna's bubblegum music is culturally important, but less important than her stance, molded by gay men and infused with a shallow awesomeness that is irresistible.

The MTV Music Video Awards in September 2003 presented an ideal moment that captured Madonna's appeal for gay and straight audiences. In honor of the twentieth anniversary of Madonna's first appearance on the MTV awards, Britney Spears and Christina Aguilera popped out of a wedding cake and writhed around in slutty wedding dresses while singing "Like a Virgin." Madonna herself then emerged dressed as a groom and tongue-kissed both of them. What a feast for gay and straight men alike! Gay men got to see Madonna pass the torch, as it were, to Christina and Britney, junior divas, while heterosexual guys could just groove on their number-one fantasy, lesbian sex, on prime-time television.

Another gay-inspired pop-music institution is the boy band. From the Beatles to the Monkees and on to Menudo and New Kids on the Block, very young all-male bands have always had a certain homoeroticism about them. Jonathan Murray, openly gay cocreator of MTV's *The Real World*, who later went on to become executive producer of *Making the Band*, told *The Advocate* in 2000, "I think I had a crush on Davy Jones. But I kept that to myself."

"One of the contradictions of the boy-band business is that it employs a large number of gay men—singers, managers, stylists—to create a product aimed at small girls," wrote Caroline Sullivan in Britain's *The Guardian* in 1999. "Most bands got their early experience playing gay clubs, whose contribution is so significant that the biggest groups, such as Five, still do Saturday-night PAs at the GAY disco in London's Charing Cross Road."

In 1999, Stephen Gately, a singer in the wildly popular British group Boyzone, announced that he was gay and had a steady boyfriend. The confession did not affect the band's sales in Britain, but some say it harmed the possibility of success in the United States. Other pop-music critics familiar with cultural differences say that none of the current crop of Brit boy bands has crossed over because their songs do not fit the patterns of the simpler tunes by the Backstreet Boys, 'N Sync, or 98 Degrees.

The American boy bands have long realized their sexual appeal to gay fans. As early as 2000, the Backstreet Boys appeared in a picture layout in the gay youth magazine *XY*. Justin Timberlake, now solo but formerly of 'N Sync, gave an interview to *Out* magazine and has publicly acknowledged his gay fans.

The tradition of gay men molding the sexual and musical tastes of adolescent girls is one thing that makes our country great. Who knows "cute boys" better—gay men or teenage girls? Many of the editors of teen celebrity magazines are openly gay guys. And now that homophobia is dissipating, adolescent gay boys can come out and say that they have crushes on boy bands, too.

Heavy Metal Was Gay, Dude!

At first glance, the world of heavy-metal rock in the 1980s seems to ooze with testosterone. It was a world for bad boys who worshipped the devil and tried to eat flying bats. They rode motorcycles, brandished chains, and liked their chicks tough. Their guitars seemed like phallic extensions of their leather-clad, beer-swilling selves. The bands had tough names such as T. Rex, Black Sabbath, Guns N' Roses, Motorhead, and Shotgun Messiah. They had legions of teenage male fans who looked up to these bands as macho role models.

Yet these heavy-metal musicians also sported eyeshadow and eyeliner. Kenneth Quinnell, a Florida political science professor, catalogs the effeminacy of what he calls "hair metal" in his humorous web essay "Heavy Metal is Gay":

Long teased hair filled with hairspray. Tight pants made
of black leather or spandex. No shirt or a black leather vest
and no shirt. Thigh-high boots. Studded belts. Make-up.
If that description doesn't describe a gay look, then it
surely describes a heterosexual transvestite look.

Quinnell doesn't stop at looks—he scrutinizes content, too, jesting that the bands are named after either phallic imagery (Tool, Prong, Mr. Big) or girls (Alice Cooper, Lizzie Borden, Twisted Sister). He mentions suspiciously homoerotic songs, such as "Falling in Love (Is Hard on the Knees)" (Aerosmith) or "Just a Gigolo" (David Lee Roth). Finally, he rests his very funny case while analyzing the performance of heavy-metal bands. Their vocals: "Big-haired queens prancing around on stage, singing cheesy pop love songs in voices that often reach high notes worthy of Mariah Carey or Whitney Houston." Their choreography: "Could these guys act more gay—wiggling around on stage, dancing in ways that straight men don't dance?" Concludes Quinnell, "Is it a coincidence that the head-banging motion just happens to be the same motion as providing oral sex to a guy?"

Quinnell was surprised by the furor his light, funny essay set off on his webzine, which is called "T. Rex's Guide to Life," in homage to the heavy-metal band T. Rex. He received scores of letters hurling nasty epithets his way: "gay sicko," "rapist serial killer," "she-man." It seems that some rabidly heterosexual fans of heavy metal don't like to think about even a *hint* of homosexual influence in their favorite rock music genre.

Quinnell, thirty-one, is a married father who teaches at Tallahassee Community College. "I've been a fan of heavy metal as long as I can remember and am actually a big fan of most of the bands I'm making fun of," he told me. "I am straight, but am always bothered by homophobia. I think, at times, the homophobia associated with heavy metal is little more than a front masking a latent or closeted homosexuality. Other times it is real homophobia, as the responses to my essay have shown."

Although Quinnell floated his essay as a joke, there are others who have identified the homo undercurrent in heavy-metal music in a more serious fashion. As early as 1972, the self-styled dean of rock critics, Robert Christgau, wrote openly in *Newsday* about the gay influences in heavy rock:

> *It's curious that the American "English hard-rock" bands are also the only American bands with an explicit connection to homosexuality—Alice Cooper through Alice's since-abandoned transvestitism, not to mention his assumed name, and the Velvets through the Warhol superstars. In England such connections are commonplace, from Mick Jagger's androgynousness and Ray Davies's camping all the way to David Bowie . . .*

Now that we are twenty years beyond the heyday of glam-rock and heavy metal, it's easier to see the "homoeroticism in metal music" as Jon Ginoli, head of the all-gay band Pansy Division, described it to a reporter in 1997. He and his band-mates took credit for helping Rob Halford, the lead singer of Judas Priest, come out of the closet that year. It was one of those "say it isn't so" moments for Generation X, I'm sure.

How could such a tough guy band be gay around the edges, or, indeed, at its core? Judas Priest, considered one of the essential heavy-metal bands of the eighties, sold millions of albums and had a hardcore heterosexual teen audience.

In Rob Halford's first interview as an "out" homosexual, he talked to *The Advocate* about his gayness and his time with Judas Priest. Unlike many gay entertainers, Halford never pretended to have girlfriends. He said that the other members of Judas Priest were aware of his sexual orientation. They would have to be, I'd think, by the look he created for the band.

"The imagery I created was simply out of a feeling that what I was doing before the leather and studs and whips and chains and motorcycles didn't fit me," said Halford. "Priest was going onstage in very flamboyant saggy pants. It was very extroverted and fluffy in its visual tone, but I didn't feel right."

So Halford went to a gay S&M shop to buy outfits for the band. It felt, he said, "right," even though he realized the irony of outfitting himself and fellow musicians in homosexual leather gear. "OK, I'm a gay man," Halford says he thought, "and I'm into leather and that sexual side of the leather world—and I'm gonna bring that onto the stage." No one seemed to notice the gay overtones at the time. Halford had unwittingly borrowed from a gay aesthetic that appealed enormously to tough heterosexual men. They loved his handcuffs, whip, chains, and especially his motorcycle. The motorcycle look, which started in blue-collar heterosexual communities in the 1950s, had soon after been adopted in gay circles. In the eighties, the leather look passed into the straight world again with a vengeance and was a favorite of teenagers everywhere. Halford was part of the great homosexual/heterosexual circle of life, bringing to his straight audiences a gay twist on a straight standard.

The sports world has adopted a new anthem in the last few years, Queen's "We Will Rock You." It was featured in the Disney *Mighty Ducks* hockey movies and is sung at hundreds of sporting events all across the country. The 2004 Super Bowl Pepsi commercial with Britney Spears in a gladiator suit featured the song, as did *Miracle*, the movie about the 1980 U.S. Olympic hockey team win. With its hand-clapping, footstomping, and rhythmic chanting, "We Will Rock You" has become far more popular than "Take Me Out to the Ballgame" or "The Boys Are Back in Town." Yet how many heterosexual sports fans, as they shout the song at the top of their lungs, realize that it was written by a gay man?

Freddie Mercury, lead singer of Queen, has been described by critics as "the Cecil B. DeMille of rock." When he announced on November 21, 1991, that he had AIDS and then died on November 24, his fans were stunned. He had kept his disease a secret, as well as his sexuality. Mercury was born to Persian parents in Zanzibar, off the Tanzanian coast, in September 1946. He started off life as Far as Faroukh Bulsara and attended boarding school in India. If Mercury hadn't been born during the rock-music era, he probably would have been a composer of opera or show tunes. Certainly, both forms showed up in his work. His brilliant song "Bohemian Rhapsody" makes fun of operatic and theatrical conventions, with shouts of "Scaramouche, Scaramouche!" and trilling arias.

And yet another one of his hits was the very Old Western, macho-sounding "Another One Bites the Dust."

Mercury was a fascinating character, very influential in the development of the rock song, and a poster fixture in many a heterosexual teen's bedroom.

Queen was inducted into the Rock and Roll Hall of Fame ten years after Freddie Mercury's death. An off-Broadway show about Mercury's life opened in January 2004: *Mercury: The Afterlife and Times of a Rock God*. Scripted and directed by Charles Messina, the one-man play focuses on Mercury's emotional struggles as a closeted performer. The actor playing Freddie Mercury dons his different "looks" throughout, and the performance costumes alone tell a story about Mercury's path as a gay man. At the beginning of Queen's career, he had dressed very flamboyantly (he was the band member who had suggested their name) in effeminate costumes, and then, when the more masculine, mustachioed look became prominent in the gay community, he adapted completely. He wore extremely tight, faded jeans, skimpy tank tops, and eighties-style aviator glasses. Or, as one of my gay friends put it, Mercury's new clothes screamed "gay, gay, gay!" Amazingly, the straight boys who made up most of his audience copied his look. (And so goes the circle of clothes—see the fashion chapter.)

When asked if he had ever socialized with Freddie Mercury, Rob Halford of Judas Priest recalled only one time, at a gay bar in Athens, Greece, where the two rockers met unexpectedly. It's amazing to think that two closet queens were able to drive all-American teenage boys into macho frenzies.

Chapter 10

Theater:
Life Is a Drag

There's a place for us,
Somewhere a place for us.

—"Somewhere," from *West Side Story*
by Stephen Sondheim

Is a gay play a play that has sex with other plays?

—Harvey Fierstein

If at the end you want them to cheer
Keep it gay, keep it gay, keep it gay,
Whether it's Hamlet, Othello or Lear,
Keep it gay, keep it gay, keep it gay!

—lyrics from *The Producers* by Mel Brooks

The only times I really feel the presence of God are when I'm having sex, and during a great Broadway musical.

—Father Dan in *Jeffrey* by Paul Rudnick

You're all flops. I am the Earth Mother, and you are all flops.

—Martha in *Who's Afraid of Virginia Woolf?*
by Edward Albee

December 2003. My daughter and I have just left a spectacular performance of a one-man play, *I Am My Own Wife* by Doug Wright. On a spare set, Jefferson Mays eerily conjures up the main role of Charlotte von Mahlsdorf, a gay transvestite furniture and clock collector in East Germany in the 1960s. Yet he also plays the role of the gay playwright, who wants to know how an obviously gay man survived the Nazis and then the incredibly repressive regime of the communists. And he portrays a gay "trick," a flamboyantly gay clock dealer, a straight military guy, and several others. It's a virtuoso performance, a great big gay stew of a theater piece. We're dazzled, or should I say dazed? We've completed a theater bender in which we've seen three plays in two days, and everything we've seen has been gay.

As we leave the theater, we walk up 45th Street, past the theater where *The Boy from Oz* is playing. It's a musical about Peter Allen, a composer who was gay but once married to Liza Minnelli. (Insert your own Liza Minnelli/she always marries gay guys/David Gest jokes here.) I beg my kid to stop in front of the theater so we can read the reviews. It's then that a middle-age gay couple approaches. One is short and a bit stout; the other is tall and balding.

"That show is fantastic!" the short guy says. "You've got to see it." I say that we've just come from *I Am My Own Wife*. They have, too. They continue to rave about *The Boy from Oz*. I mention that most reviews say it's not a good play, but that Hugh Jackman is supposed to be incredible in the lead role. It's clear that mentioning anything negative about the show makes them angry. The show is perfect, they say, and most enjoyable.

The taller of the couple asks if we saw *Taboo*, the Boy George musical. "Yeah, but we kind of didn't like it," I say, and then they lose interest in us entirely. But our dislike is not because of its gay theme, I tell them. The musical's got a weak book. (Well, I could mention that the scene featuring copulation in a men's john was a little . . . off-center for a mainstream Broadway audience, but I don't.)

The couple goes away, because I've obviously offended them. Their comments have implied that when something is gay, it is always good. Of course that's not true. But I'm just delighted to be able to discuss three plays with gay themes that are now mainstream. Gone are the days when a play like *The Boys in the Band* caused a ruckus. (And also gone are the times when gay men could only be depicted as raving, suicidal lunatics who would rather be straight.)

When *Falsettoland*, William Finn's gay musical about a man and his son, came to Broadway in 1992, the producers deliberately ran ads featuring wholesome families who raved about how touching and wholesome the musical was. (Translation: Don't be scared of the gay boys!)

But now straight people no longer have to be coaxed into gay productions like frightened horses. Gay is good. Gay is funny. Gay is safe. *Hairspray,* the raucous musical, is based on gay director John Waters's movie of the same name and stars Harvey Fierstein in drag as the main character's mother. The 2003 Tony Award for best play went to *Take Me Out,* about a major-league baseball player who reveals that he's homosexual. *Mamma Mia!,* the ABBA-based musical, is very gay— first, because so many gay men adore ABBA songs, and second, because there is a gay twist in the plot.

And, of course, many—or most—of the audience members watching these shows are straight. Finally, the great secret of the theater has come out of the closet: The best theater is gay, or at least embraces gay themes. And straight people are now flocking to the theater to see very explicitly homosexual material. Of course, there is always the nagging question: Is it just a minstrel show? From the 1920s to the 1940s, white audiences flocked to Harlem to see black performers. Is the straight pilgrimage to gay plays an echo of that practice?

Out of the three plays my daughter and I see on our theater-bender weekend, *Avenue Q* seems to be the least likely to contain gay elements. *Avenue Q* is a spoof of *Sesame Street,* but it's so much more. It follows a group of people and puppets who are young, just out of college, and forced to live in a seedy neighborhood in one of the outer boroughs of New York.

It's a delightful show. I'm a cynic, but I find myself laughing and crying at these characters' situations. And there's a major gay subplot—concerning Bert- and Ernie-like characters. It's wonderful and sly, a pop-culture reference to the constant speculation about *Sesame Street's* Bert and Ernie's sexual preferences. (Why do they sleep in the same room, and why are they always together?) In *Avenue Q,* the Bert-like character, Rod, confesses a terrible crush on the Ernie-like puppet, Nicky. Yet Rod, who spends most of the musical declaring that he is not gay, sings a very funny song about why no one ever sees him with a girlfriend—he has a girlfriend in Canada. In the end, after much therapy, Rod comes out of the closet and Nicky finds him a lover, a cousin who looks just like Nicky but is a gay bodybuilder. (The puppet version of a gay gymrat is hilarious, with all his muscles molded out of foam.)

Queer Theater: A Redundant Term?

Okay, let's identify the "hidden" gay influences on straight theater.

Wait—whom am I kidding? Maybe this chapter is superfluous. The term "straight theater" just might be oxymoronic. All theater is essentially queer, because of its emphasis on artifice, social exaggeration, and gender play. Think of the giant phalluses in the choruses of Greek comedies. Consider that it's a form in which men played *all* the roles for centuries. Yes, Shakespeare played around with sexual identity. And perhaps, from the little we know about his personal life and his plays and sonnets, Shakespeare might have found young men to be the most suitable erotic objects.

So, by the Lenny Bruce standard, all actors are queer, even if they are straight. All theater producers and directors are gay. The proscenium stage is gay, and so, especially, is the *thrust* stage.

I could argue that the theater is at best a marginal art form these days, reaching few people. But that's not exactly true. For one thing, the plays that stick around on Broadway eventually make their way to far-flung cities via road troupes. Then, later, those same plays are made into movies or television events. Both *The Producers* and *Hairspray* are to be made into films; ironically, each production started out as a film. So, even though only a tiny percent of Americans make it to the Great White Way, we are constantly being influenced by the legitimate theater's offshoots. And then, of course, there are the classic American plays performed by high-school and community theater groups around the country. Many of these were written by gay men.

Surprises in the Backstage Closet

The one I couldn't believe was Thornton Wilder. It was another Liberace moment for me—my literary gaydar had never gone off. I knew that Wilder had never married, but it never occurred to me that he was gay. How could the playwright who wrote the wholesome American classic *Our Town* be a closeted homosexual? Yet there he was on an Internet list of gay playwrights. Now, that listing doesn't necessarily mean that he was gay. But biographers seem to conclude he was at least possibly a homosexual. He's even claimed as queer by the "Gay Bears" of the UC Berkeley campus. (Wilder grew up in Berkeley. His mother was obsessed with culture; his father was often away at diplomatic posts in Asia.) Thornton Wilder seems to have had only one male lover in his life, and probably no one else, male *or* female. That's sad. I wish he'd experienced more real-life passion.

I called a couple heterosexual friends with theater backgrounds who had never known, either. The man with whom Wilder might have had a brief affair (maybe as brief as one sexual encounter) was Samuel Steward, provocatively described on one gay site as "university professor, writer, tattoo artist, [and] pornographer." Steward wrote erotic novels under the name Phil Andros and, along with Wilder, was friends with Gertrude Stein. One of Wilder's biographers, Gilbert Harrison (*The Enthusiast: A Life of Thornton Wilder*) wrote in 1983 that Steward described sex with Thornton Wilder as "so hurried and reticent, so barren of embrace, tenderness or passion that it might never have happened." Harrison reports that according to Steward's comments, Wilder found the act of man-on-man sex "unspeakable."

In his book *The United States*, a paranoid Gore Vidal praises Thornton Wilder's writing abilities, along with his ability to remain in the closet: "Fortunately for Wilder's reputation, he was able to keep his private life relatively secret."

Thinking about this hidden aspect of Thornton Wilder's

personality is like watching the movie *Blue Velvet,* in which
Kyle MacLachlan finds a human ear in a perky, "normal" suburban field. Under the utter wholesomeness of Wilder's
hometown dramas lurks a dark, alienated side. There is always premature death and unfulfilled longing. His one-act,
The Long Christmas Dinner, depicts several generations of one
family going slowly and steadily through portals of life and
into death. The breeders among the characters never fare
well—the maiden aunts are always smarter than the married
couples. And he does portray tortured, sexually ambivalent
characters. In the Pulitzer Prize–winning *Our Town* (1938),
Simon Stimson, the town drunk and organist for the Congre-
gational Church in Grovers Corners, commits suicide. Some
have said that he represents a closeted gay man destroyed by
life in a small town.

Even if Thornton Wilder had never been outed, we would
still have to count him as a pivotal figure in gay theater history. Adapting a German play into his popular stage hit *The
Matchmaker,* he created the famous character of Dolly Levi,
later to become a gay icon in the musical *Hello, Dolly!,* with
music by the divinely gay Jerry Herman. That's true homo-
power.

Why were gay men so adept at exploring the American
melodrama? William Inge is another gay playwright who remained closeted and yet produced several classics of heterosexual longing set in the small-town environment. I studied
lots of his plays in high school, as many of us baby boomers
did. Inge's characters spoke to me. I related, in particular, to
his young female characters, who were always struggling with

their sexuality. But I never would have dreamed that he was homosexual.

Inge had four huge hits on Broadway: *Come Back, Little Sheba* (1950), *Picnic* (1953), *Bus Stop* (1955), and *The Dark at the Top of the Stairs* (1957). All were rather agonizing melodramas that got turned into popular Hollywood films. Another original screenplay of his, for *Splendor in the Grass* (1961), starring Natalie Wood and Warren Beatty, is, along with *Rebel Without a Cause*, a classic of the prototype teen flick. Natalie Wood is a girl who isn't good enough for her boyfriend, and so her shallow boyfriend betrays her with another girl. I remember seeing it on television and identifying with the acute sense of alienation of Natalie's character. Perhaps, because of the essential level of alienation being closeted entails, Inge was able to infuse a female character with a gay, sensitive level of articulation. Although he never came out officially, much later in life he wrote several unproduced plays with homosexual characters and themes. Yet Nebraska Wesleyan theater scholar Jay Scott Chipman believes that even Inge's closeted plays "could benefit from careful gay analysis." He cites the playwright's constant emphasis on sexuality, athleticism and muscle culture, and his constant, "incisive critique of heterosexual domesticity and desire. . . ."

When it comes down to it, the genre of the post–World War II Broadway melodrama was practically all gay-driven. As John M. Clum notes in his book *Still Acting Gay*:

> *Three of the four most critically acclaimed and commercially successful playwrights of the postwar period were*

> *closeted homosexuals whose plays were supported by the*
> *critical establishment so long as they maintained the con-*
> *ventions of closet drama. Of the pantheon of Tennessee*
> *Williams, William Inge, Edward Albee, and Arthur Miller,*
> *only Miller was heterosexual. . . . In the 1950s, Broad-*
> *way was still the venue for serious drama. . . . Williams,*
> *Albee, and Inge had to negotiate between their experi-*
> *ence as homosexual men and the conventions of popular*
> *drama.*

This blows my mind—that straight America was watching plays and movies created about their culture by gay men who could not even admit to being a part of their own uniquely creative and sexually exciting outsider culture. When I read Tennessee Williams's first play, *The Glass Menagerie*, I saw it as a drama about family dynamics and failed heterosexual love. And that is what, as a part of a mass, straight audience, I was supposed to see. But some of my gay friends who read it in their teens saw Tom, the overly sensitive brother, as a homosexual with romantic yearnings for the gentleman caller he's brought to meet his sister, Laura.

The attributes that the fifties female wanted in a man—that he be a man's man, someone who was a bit rough around the edges and could sweep her off her feet—were created by homosexual writers who wanted the same thing. "Tennessee Williams invented the homosexual," said one wag at a conference I attended. The hot look of Marlon Brando dressed in a white "wife beater" T-shirt (as he was in *Streetcar Named Desire*) or in a leather motorcycle jacket, was a very fifties homo-

sexual look that had started crossing over to the straight population. In an interview, gay drama professor Bud Coleman
from the University of Colorado told me of his theory that it
was Tennessee Williams who made it safe for America to eroti-
cize the male body. In his plays, it was often the men who were
the sex objects, such as Stanley Kowalski in *Streetcar*, or Brick in
Cat on a Hot Tin Roof. And it was in Williams's plays that men
strutted center-stage in skimpy pajamas or with bare chests.

Of the three gay major playwrights I've mentioned, it was
Williams who ultimately felt the most comfortable with, and
was the earliest to begin discussing, his homosexuality. (Although he once declared to a newspaper reporter, "Brick Pollitt
[of *Cat on a Hot Tin Roof*] is *not* a homosexual!") But as early as
1970, Williams gave a lengthy interview to David Frost in
which he discussed being gay. Edward Albee is now "out" but
seems to resent having to talk about his homosexuality at all.

I acted in a really stupid high-school production of Albee's
one-act play *The Sandbox*. I played Grandma, who was waiting
for the Angel of Death, who just happened to be played by a
muscle-bound half-naked guy (not a pretty sight in our drama
club). It's an absurdist play, one of those where the characters
don't have names and prattle on endlessly about the meaning of
life. Well, not prattle. They utter monosyllabic and disjointed
dialogue. We high-schoolers really didn't understand it, and I
kept wondering why death came in the form of a gorgeous
young man with muscles in a skimpy bikini. Now I know.

In 2001, I stayed after a performance of Albee's off-
Broadway production *The Play About the Baby* to hear him
answer questions from the audience. One person asked whether

all his characters were really gay, even if they were presented as heterosexuals. Albee became furious. He told the audience about how one theater company had acquired the rights to do his play *Who's Afraid of Virginia Woolf?* with an all-male cast. "If I had wanted to write about homosexuals, I would have!" he bellowed.

But *Who's Afraid of Virginia Woolf?*, his most naturalistic play, was first produced in 1962. Back then, could Albee have written a play about a group of sniping homosexuals and get it produced on Broadway? I doubt it, in the closeted mid-sixties. Yet the sometimes surrealistic, bitchy view of human relationships in *Who's Afraid of Virginia Woolf?* has a genuine gay sensibility anyway, even if it is voiced through heterosexual couples.

Ironically, the true heirs to Albee's aggressive unnaturalistic style, peppered with staccato dialogue, have all been heterosexual playwrights—Sam Shepard (*Buried Child, True West, Fool for Love*), David Rabe (*Streamers, Hurlyburly*); John Guare (*The House of Blue Leaves*), and David Mamet (*American Buffalo, Glengarry Glen Ross*). This is another case of heterosexuals borrowing from homosexual innovators.

Mae West, the Drag Queen's Queen, or the Great Imitator of the Great White Way

"I used to be Snow White, but I drifted" was my all-time favorite line when I was going through my W. C. Fields/Mae

West phase as a teenager. Of course, Mae has become a great gay icon, an even more exaggerated version of a blonde bomb than Harlow, Marilyn, or Doris Day. My grandfather, who died before I was born, was a big fan of hers, but my mom could never understand why. "To me, she was so exaggerated," Mom says. "Kind of creepy, so artificial and almost like a man."

My mom was on to something, because in the history of Broadway, Mae West is famous for being the first to put homosexuals on stage, and for trying to put drag queens up there, too. West's first show, *Sex,* in 1928, had gay characters, and her next one, *The Drag,* closed out of town in Paterson, N.J.

West got much of her inspiration from vaudeville and gay-club drag queens. She is said to have borrowed her classic hip-swaying walk and other mannerisms from Bert Savoy, a drag entertainer extraordinaire. Now here's that homo "circle of life" thing again—Mae West, a woman, imitating a man who was imitating a woman, and arousing my grandfather in the process.

Musicals, the Great American Homo Art Form

There is nothing else like the Broadway musical. It's a peculiar American form, inextricably linked with the creative abilities of gay men. And gay men have served as stewards, as keepers of the faith, even when everyone had predicted, year after year, that the musical was dead.

"For gay believers, musicals are what football is to many

straight men," says John Kenrick, a historian and former theater manager. "We relish souvenirs and statistics, root wildly for our favorites, and know all too well the difference between a winning season and a losing one. They have the Super Bowl—we have Tony Award night."

I talked with Kenrick, whose enthusiasm about musical theater is boundless. He thinks that musicals have always appealed to the gay sensibility, and have been shaped by it, because gay men have always wanted a perfect world, "a world where you can get up on a table and dance and sing, and everything is suddenly okay."

Kenrick consults with museums about musical-theater exhibits. He also runs a website, Musicals101.com, which is the most comprehensive site about Broadway I've ever encountered. It was from Kenrick that I learned, with the source verified, that Winston Churchill had once slept with Ivor Novello, a gay English matinee idol. When asked how it was, Churchill said, "Very musical!"

Kenrick points out that "the Broadway musical and the term 'homosexuality' were invented almost simultaneously." The year was 1866, when a lively play, *The Black Crook,* debuted in New York. That same year, the German Karl Ulrichs publicly defined his attraction to his own sex as "urning," and a year later, also in Germany, the term "homosexual" appeared in print for the first time. "A coincidence," says John Kenrick, "but one that theater queens can delight in."

I'm interested in dramatic and musical watersheds. It's great to think about what strides were being made, say, in the 1970s, with musicals such as *A Chorus Line* featuring gay characters and gay situations. And *The Boys in the Band* was a totally gay play, even if it did succumb to some very negative gay stereotypes. Yet in terms of how gay composers and playwrights affected straight America, I'm much more interested in the musicals written and produced by closeted gay men in the 1950s and early 1960s.

Men such as Leonard Bernstein, Arthur Laurents, Jerome Robbins, and Stephen Sondheim changed the direction of the American musical forever. In works such as *Candide, West Side Story, Gypsy, Company,* and *Follies,* they recreated the American musical as a fluid, socially conscious art form with realistic characters and choreography that incorporated dance techniques from different cultures. Entire books have been written about the genesis of *West Side Story,* a 1959 gay collaboration that seemed made in heaven. The homosexual actor Montgomery Clift had asked Jerome Robbins how he might best play a Hispanic Romeo in a film he was considering; from that small question came the idea for writing a musical based on *Romeo and Juliet* and yet set amid the backdrop of a gang-infested Puerto Rican neighborhood in contemporary New York. Bernstein wrote the soaring melodies for songs that have become romantic standards ("Somewhere," "Tonight"), as well as novelty numbers that sounded as if they had been overheard on the streets ("Officer Krupke," "In America"). Sondheim and Laurents supplied the hip lyrics and book, while Robbins provided the liveliest, most streetwise choreography ever seen on Broadway.

As usual, the gay collaborators were well ahead of their time: Theater scholars point out that *West Side Story* lost out in the Tony Awards to *The Music Man,* a much more conventional show. Yet the gay sensibility that shaped *West Side Story* would in the end begin to pervade the mainstream Broadway show. Stephen Sondheim has always bristled when asked if "Somewhere" is truly a gay song about the yearning to belong. Yet the song has become an anthem for gay pride, in part, I think, because the sense of alienation so vital to the gay aesthetic practically oozes from *West Side Story.* In the history of the theater, this show, with its poignant songs of longing and rebellion, is the first moment when the gay vision addressed another alienated group: the youth of a prejudiced America.

Stephen and Tony and Mainstream American Theater

The wonderful 2003 teen movie *Camp* opens as summer theater students board the bus for Camp Ovation, an upstate New York outpost where they will star in musicals and plays. In a deliciously comic riff, the campers on the bus begin singing the torch song "Losing My Mind," from Stephen Sondheim's *Follies.* In scene after scene, the movie features mostly gay boys and ugly-duckling girls singing Sondheim songs way over their heads. In one audition, six awkward thirteen-year-olds warble another world-weary *Follies* song, "I'm Still Here."

Sondheim, a gay man who admits that it took him until his seventies to fall in love, has come to symbolize the future of the American musical. When, in the film, he shows up at Camp Ovation in a cameo appearance, the queer kid performers go crazy—it's as if Shaquille O'Neal had suddenly turned up at a basketball camp.

Although Sondheim's most recent Broadway productions have been less than successful, his gay vision has forever influenced straight theater tastes. Yet, as of this writing, the revival of his dark musical *Assassins* is finding an enthusiastic audience. In choosing exotic material such as the story of washed-up showgirls (*Follies*), an Ingmar Bergman film (*A Little Night Music*), the coming of westerners to Japan (*Pacific Overtures*), or a mythic London murderer (*Sweeney Todd*), he pushed the envelope in mainstream theater tastes. He made audiences think and influenced later composers and lyricists, gay and straight. Jonathan Larson's *Rent,* for example, owes its lineage more to Sondheim than Puccini. Sondheim created the more operatic musical, eschewing the big showstopping scores of an earlier time.

Some critics have gone so far as to say that Sondheim's musicals are meta-musicals about homosexuality itself. He says no, and I agree with him. And yet he brings with him a certain style that is definitely post-homosexual, an effete and witty effect that hasn't been seen much since Cole Porter. He has even succeeded in writing a poignant torch song, "Send In the Clowns," that is seriously performed everywhere (even by folksinger Judy Collins) but has also become a camp classic.

The greatest gay playwrights of the waning days of the twentieth century—Stephen Sondheim and Tony Kushner—

are no longer considered "gay." Similarly, Arthur Miller is no longer considered a "Jewish" playwright, as he was in the 1950s. Sondheim and Kushner have something in common with Miller: They refuse to be confined by sexuality or ethnicity. They aspire to be American playwrights with big ideas, and they have achieved that goal.

Tony Kushner, in particular, presents a new convergence of gay and straight themes in his work. His two-part *Angels in America* took Broadway by storm in the early nineties. Set within a large landscape populated by gay and straight characters, and accessing themes and emotions from Christianity, Judaism, the Cold War, and the AIDS epidemic, Kushner's epic play was a synthesis of American themes that had been left unraveled for decades. Kushner is a playwright who likes to tackle large social constructs. He helped Anna Deveare Smith arrange the material for *Twilight: Los Angeles,* her vivid set of monologues about the Los Angeles riots of 1992. A more recent play, *Homebody/Kabul,* is an eloquent examination of the differences between Western culture and a third-world Afghanistan. *Caroline, or Change,* an operetta about race set at the time of the Kennedy assassination, has been praised for its innovative form. No wonder *The New York Times* recently dubbed him "Hurricane Kushner."

If there was any doubt that Kushner's gay sensibility could play to straight Middle America beyond Broadway, it was disbursed by the lavish production HBO gave to *Angels in America,* directed by Mike Nichols. *Angels* was *the* event of the Fall 2003 season, featuring true movie stars Meryl Streep, Al Pacino, and Emma Thompson. The play, which had debuted in the spring of 1993, seemed not to have aged over a decade but rather to have deepened in its relevance. In its original subtitle, Kushner had dubbed the piece "A Gay Fantasia on National Themes." The play seems less particularly gay now and more about how individuals cope with national and personal tragedy. In the aftermath of the enormous loss of 9/11, *Angels* became a comforting play about the strength and diversity of the American character. Here, finally, we had a gay vision, obsessed with the horrible AIDS scourge, interpreting loss and renewal in American culture. Here we had Roy Cohn, vicious anti-Communist lawyer, laid bare by a deadly disease that revealed his own homosexuality, and yet still unable to integrate his sexuality with his life or his eventual fate.

The success of Kushner's play on Broadway and its enormously popular cable television production were signs as sure as the signs of the coughing angel in his script: America is looking to groups that once were considered fringe or "evil"— i.e., homosexuals—to explain the stressful turn of current events. Harper, the lonely Mormon wife in *Angels in America* who discovers that her husband is a homosexual and that her faith is waning, speaks about loss and love at the end of the second part of the play, "Perestroika." She seems to be describing all of American history: "Nothing's lost forever. In this world, there is a kind of painful progress. Longing for what we've left behind, and dreaming ahead."

Living
in a Gay Time:
Homos "Я" Us

I don't want to look to the past and romanticize it . . . but gay men used to be a bastion of culture and refinement. Not that you have to dress up in little scarves or even go to the opera necessarily, but I feel we're losing that culture.

—singer Rufus Wainwright

I should like to know why nearly every man that approaches greatness tends towards homosexuality, whether he admits it or not.

—D. H. Lawrence

I'm a girly man. There's a whole group of us, the Girly Man's Club—Gary Oldman, Frank Langella, Geoffrey

Rush—all enthusiastically heterosexual men who are bored by sports and would much rather go shopping.

—actor Alfred Molina

[Q]ueerdom was a country in which there was more fun. There was something about homosexuality that seemed too much, too gorgeous, too ripe. I later came to realize that there was something marvelous about it because it seemed to be pushing everything to its fullest point.

—artist Larry Rivers, praising the gay art world of the 1950s

There was a much-used adage during the feminist movement of the 1970s: "Ginger Rogers did everything Fred Astaire did, but backwards *and* in high heels." When I look at what gay men have accomplished in our world, I think: *Homosexuals did everything with great style and panache, and they did a lot of it in tiny closets with no lights, and sometimes while fearing for their lives.*

The amazing richness gay men have contributed to our culture can't be denied—yet hardly anyone in straight America has acknowledged it on the grand scale it demands. And gay men should also get points for extra effort. They've given of themselves while always living within a largely homophobic culture and while coping with a devastating disease that continues to make horrible inroads into their communities.

I know it will take a long time for America to become a truly homophilic society, but the signs are here. Queer television is expanding. Gay marriages are now acknowledged in two states, and the stuffy *New York Times* finally prints homosexual marriage announcements. We see more gay elected officials every year, and more "out" businesspeople. The brave mayor of San Francisco, Gavin Newsom, recently went out on a limb to perform thousands of same-sex marriages not sanctioned by California's existing laws.

Gays are gradually being assimilated into mainstream culture, and therefore are at the point where their uniqueness as a people will inevitably become threatened. If they're not careful, they could become boring, just like straight people.

I hope that doesn't happen. I hope that with more widespread acceptance, gay men will continue to bring their verve and flamboyance to the mainstream. After all, it's hip to be gay. Heterosexuals envy the gay lifestyle, with its disposable income, innate stylishness, frequent travel, and stimulating nightlife.

"The Love That Dare Not Speak Its Name" has always whispered on the fringes of our straight world, making quiet suggestions for a more civilized way of life. Now that voice is singing and talking at normal volume. Straight people can hear that steady hum of change and recognize that it has been there all along. In the end, this era, with its emphasis on artifice, consumerism, and emotional narcissism, is a very gay time. In the end, I think it is truer than anyone realizes: *We are all homosexuals.* Or at the very least, as we embrace the gay aesthetic, we seem to be echoing Flaubert's sentiments about his own conflicted character, Emma Bovary: "Homo, c'est moi."

Acknowledgments

Thanks to all of the people who shared anecdotes, information, and encouragement.

The first serious debts of gratitude must be paid to my daughter, Kelly Forman Crimmins, the Junior Goddess and Hag-Fag, and to my mother, Betty Kelly Crimmins Lancaster, the Senior Goddess and Soother. They keep me going, that's for sure, and so does Alan Forman, who has been a great support over the years.

I'd also like to thank my late father, David J. Crimmins, a man ahead of his time, who long ago explained male homosexuality to me while expertly quoting the Kinsey report.

Help arrived in astounding forms, and always right when I needed it, from my beloved friends and family: Sarah Babaian,

Alexandra Mower, Robin Warshaw, Jimmy Schank, Anne Kaier, Barry Bergen, Joanne Babaian, Ronnie Polanezcky, Charisse Savarin, Stephanie Kahn, Kathy Romine, and Mark Richard.

Many people were generous with time and interviews, including Nelson Aspen, Philip Gerson, John Kenrick, Luke Yankee, Sam Pancake, Gary Gates, Jeremy Wintroub, Daniel Coleridge, and Kenneth Quinnell.

My crack team of researchers included David Sinkler, Patty Quinn, Frank Garritty, and Tom O'Leary.

Joellen Brown, who's been present at the birth of all my books, was once again an excellent midwife.

In addition to his helpful music research, Frank Garrity kept me alive. My dog would have eaten my face off during the writing phase if not for Frank's help. Tom O'Leary kept me writing by passing along articles and encouragement throughout the process.

My agent, Susan Raihofer, was always most helpful and open to all my ideas. I'd also like to thank my editor, Mitch Horowitz, and my publisher, Joel Fotinos, for their patience and strong support of the book. Ashley Shelby deserves thanks for trying to make sense of my worm-ridden manuscript. Thanks also to my enthusiastic publicist, Kelly Groves.

If I've forgotten anyone, please forgive me. And please know that any errors or flaws in this book are mine, and mine alone.

Thanks, everyone!

—*Cathy Crimmins*, 2004

About the Author

Cathy Crimmins has written nineteen books, including *When My Parents Were My Age, They Were Old*, and *Curse of the Mommy*. Her most recent, *Where Is the Mango Princess?: A Journey Back from Brain Injury*, won the Outstanding Book Award from the American Society of Journalists and Authors (ASJA) and is being made into a television movie. An award-winning educational screenwriter, Crimmins speaks frequently, keynoting conferences across the country, and has taught nonfiction writing at the University of Pennsylvania. She has been the recipient of the Pennsylvania Council on the Arts Fellowship in Literature. Crimmins now lives in Los Angeles and believes that English majors will someday rule the world.